PUSH

Birthing Your Dreams Into Reality

SHERYL L. BROWN

PUSH

Birthing Your Dreams Into Reality

Pneuma Life Publishing
P.O. BOX 885
Lanham, MD 20706
www.pneumalife.com

Acknowledgements

Much love and appreciation goes to those who have spoken life into me and the dream that was birthed from my inner man. My parents, Shellie Stewart, Christine Stewart. Derwin & Kimberly Stewart. My sister, Brenda Stewart. Uncle L.J. and Aunt Frances Rodgers; Aunt Dorothy Ross; Cousin Perry Rodgers; my Godmother, Odis Tucker-Figures; Pastor Martha L. Johnson; L.B. and Doris Williams; Thomas and Linda Grant; Patrick Brown; my Mother-in-law, Ollie Brown; Nellie Wright; Opal Hooks; Mark Strother; Greg Lane Jr.; Erwin Lane; Jessie and Mary Alice Lane; Mary Ann Bryant; Elaine Street; Henry Hollis; Vicki Sykes; Vicki Coffee; Sharon Moore; Devon and Debra Edwards; Gayle Claiborne; Geri Spencer; Pastor Virgil and Geraldine Patterson; Harold and Johnny Keyes; Alvera Benson; Ruth Kelly; Robyn Fargo; Mark Garibaldi; Dr. Phil Paris; Charles West; Tommie Hollis; Harriet Edwards; Dr. Kathy Ritter; Gilda & Veronica Spencer.

Table of Contents

Dedication

I dedicate this book to my high priest, my best friend, my companion, my lover, my husband, Shawn Durelle Brown. Good things come to those who wait.

Preface

1987 was one of the most exciting years of my life. I was granted the opportunity to cross the stage at Cal State University Bakersfield and receive my bachelor's of science degree in biology. It was a well-deserved degree that consumed a lot of my time, patience, prayer and hard work. I was about to embark on another phase of my life, but little did I know that I was about to face a life-threatening event that would challenge me to go beyond the norm to survive. No degree could help me through this unwelcome situation, but it was my faith in God and the promises that are declared in God's Word that brought me through. I didn't have time for a pity party because I was down to 68 pounds and had just a few days to live during the course of dealing with a disease called tuberculosis peritonitis. For two years, I withdrew from the deposits I had made in my spirit man prior to my sickness in order to speak life into my body. I stood on God's Word every day and declared that I would live and not die. My illness became worse. The doctors in Bakersfield were unable to detect what was wrong with me the first time I was admitted into the hospital. After several tests, they told my mother there was nothing else they could do, so they sent me home. At that time, my parents couldn't afford health insurance. Yet, I did not qualify for Medi-Cal because they made too much money. We were truly between a rock and a hard place. To toughen matters, my parents were separated and contemplating divorce, and I was considered the mediator of the family and helped resolve family disputes. But during this time, everyone had to fight for himself. I was definitely fighting for myself. During the last stages of this illness, I lost some of my motor skills, and my brother had to carry me to the bathroom and to the hospital. One day my prayers became a natural manifestation. I was watching The 700 Club, and Pat Roberts said someone was experiencing healing in the intestinal area. Right then and there in my den, I felt a warmth come over my body. Shortly after experiencing a miracle in my body, my father's cousin by marriage, Mary Alice, who at the time worked at UCLA, had arranged for me to see a pediatrician. The doctor was able to detect the problem and provide the medical care I needed. Imagine a 23-year-old being seen by a pediatrician. I once heard a pastor say that we miss our blessings sometimes because we think they should come in certain packages.

I was at UCLA for almost a month, and during that time, I saw God perform miracles on my behalf. People I never met before were telling me they had been praying for me. Some of the staff members who worked on my floor were members of Crenshaw Christian Center, a.k.a. the Faith Dome. When I was discharged from the hospital, I weighed 89 pounds. I had to eat four or five times a day to regain the weight I had lost.

Because of the severity of the disease, the state of California paid all expenses and even granted me disability until I was able to go back to work. Thank God! It was during my time of rest that I started writing this book. I had time to think and reflect on my life. During that time, the following questions came to mind: Why does it seem that dreams come true some of the time? What prevents people from getting what they want all the time? And if desires are inner wants with outer works, what prevents someone's dream from becoming reality?

I believe this book will encourage you not only to go beyond the norm, but also to tap into your potential. This book will answer your questions as they relate to your dreams that have become stagnant. I believe the reason you bought this book was not just because of the title. I believe you bought this book because you are at a point in your life where you are expecting more than you are receiving. You are tired of settling. You want the best that life can offer. So ask yourself these questions: Are you tired of your dreams coming true some of the time? Are you tired of once-in-a-lifetime opportunities passing you by because you were not prepared? Are you tired of your dreams consuming your inner man and never being manifested into reality? Then this book is for you.

1 DREAMS DEFINED

It happens to you all the time. It's part of your everyday life. No matter who you are or what you've achieved in life, you dream. Sometimes big. However, if you're like many people, your dreams remain just that—dreams. But it doesn't have to be that way. Dreams really can come true. But you can't just sit back and wait for it to happen. Like giving birth to a child, birthing your dreams into reality is going to take some work. It is not always going to be easy. You'll have to push yourself to get there. But it will all be worth it because you will have fulfilled your dreams.

Before you begin birthing your dreams into reality, it is important to understand the definitions of dreams, goals and desires, and the part each plays in the dream-birthing process. Even though each concept has a distinct meaning, these terms are used interchangeably in this book when explaining the process of seeing your dreams become reality.

What Is a Dream?

A dream is a visual picture that has manifested itself into your thought process. How does a dream develop? It is your thought process, your mind, that gives you the ability to receive, register and recall information that is centered around your dream. Your mind is made up of three components: the conscious, the subconscious and the conscience. The conscious is the part of the thought process that allows you to concentrate on information that is being presented to you. For example, right now you are consciously concentrating on the information being conveyed in this book. Your conscious passes on the information to the subconscious. The subconscious, a level below the conscious, serves as a carrier and delivers information from the conscious to the conscience, your belief system.

For example, say you have always dreamed of becoming a renowned motivational speaker. You begin to listen to and associate with people, places and things that pertain to being a motivational speaker. You concentrate on motivational speakers' stage presence and the content of the material they're presenting. So you are concentrating on how to become a motivational speaker by continually exposing your mind with things that are associated with being a motivational speaker. All the information your mind has consumed has become part of you and is now stored in your conscience. I believe dreams are the byproduct of what you surround yourself with on a daily basis. Dreams are the byproduct of what you believe in and what you value most in life. What is the purpose of dreaming? People say dreams are a vision of oneself in the future. If that is the case, dreams allow you the ability to see what you are capable of becoming. What you deposit in your belief system influences how you act, talk and associate with people, things or events in your environment.

What is a Goal?

A goal is something you obtain. A goal is an expected outcome or achievement that evolves from specific actions that are centered around the dream needing to be fulfilled. What is the purpose of a goal? The purpose is threefold: 1) to assist in constantly lining up your thought process with your dream; 2) to challenge you to become something more, rather than just to be who you are; 3) to discipline you to stay on track while fulfilling your dream.

What is a Desire?

A desire is a cherished expectation you long to see manifested in your life. A desire evolves from a dream and becomes an inward possession that is constantly being exposed to a visual picture. The dream is then incorporated into your thinking process. What is the purpose of a desire? It is to exercise the potential that exists in the inner man to the point that it goes beyond what is needed to accomplish what is wanted. In other words, desires surpass your needs and go down into your wants. Desires give you the will to be all that you were meant to be. A desire will not allow you to settle for status quo. A desire looks the impossible in the face and laughs. A desire is your inner wants with outer works.

Your desires live in your inner man. The inner man is the spirit man that dwells within your physical body. You are tri-part being. You are a spirit, you live in a body, and you have a soul. Your inner man is a separate entity that operates independently from the human body. Your senses and feelings that normally influence your emotions do not have an impact on the inner man. The inner man has the unique ability to go beyond your senses and feelings and perceive a situation or a problem from a different angle. The inner man is where your will, potential, courage, endurance, determination, greatness, inner strength and desires are all wrapped into one.

Have you ever physically felt like giving up, but something on the inside of you pushes you to go on? That something is your inner man. Your physical being sets limitations, while your inner man has no boundaries. While the physical being is looking at the problem, the inner man is looking at the solution. While the physical being is always indulging in the present, the inner man is concentrating on the future. While the physical being is worrying, the inner man is planning. While the physical being is anxious, the inner man is patient. What is the purpose of your inner man? It is not only to "house" your desires, but also to serve as a liaison between you and the future.

To get a feel for the difference between a dream, a desire and a goal, imagine you are at the bottom of a staircase looking up. To be at the top of the staircase is your dream. Each step you take is a small goal and is considered the outer work. The heartfelt expectation of completing each step is a desire, or an inner want. Once you reach the top of the staircase, your goals have made your dream become reality.

Recap

1. What is a dream? A dream is visual picture that has manifested itself into your thinking process.

2. The mind, your thought process is made up of three components:

    - **Conscious**—the area of your mind that concentrates on the information being presented to you.
    - **Subconscious**—a level below the conscious that delivers the information received from the conscious to the conscience.
    - **Conscience**—your belief system.

3. What is the purpose of dreaming? It allows you to see what you are capable of becoming.

4. What is a goal? A goal is an expected outcome or achievement that evolves from specific actions that are centered around the dream needing to be fulfilled.

5. What is the purpose of a goal?

    - To assist in constantly lining up your thought process with your dream.
    - To challenge you to become something more, rather than just to be who you are.
    - To discipline you to stay on track while fulfilling your dream.

6. What is a desire? It is a cherished expectation you long to see manifested in your life.

7. What is the purpose of a desire? To exercise the potential that exists in the inner man to the point that it goes beyond what is needed to accomplish what is wanted.

8. What is the inner man? It is the spirit man that dwells within us. We are a tri-part being. We are a spirit, we live in a body, and we have a soul. The inner man is a separate entity from our physical being, and it operates independently from our senses, feelings and emotions.

9. What is the purpose of the inner man? To house your desires and to serve as a liaison between you and the future.

Notes

1. Write down your dreams.

2. Write down the goals that you will need to accomplish before your dreams can become reality.

Notes

2 Getting Organized

Before you can birth your dreams into reality, it is essential that you become organized. Becoming organized means creating a systematic method of prioritizing the elements of your life (i.e., family, finances, work schedule, etc.) to operate in an effective and efficient manner to see your dreams become reality.

Six Reasons for Being Organized

1. Organization brings peace. Having a sense of peace allows you to function properly and work in harmony with yourself to see your dream become reality. Have you ever been caught off guard by a situation for which you were unable to prepare? It can be frustrating. Frustration occurs when an individual fails to establish an environment that generates peace. Confusion can never be the byproduct of organization because confusion interferes with your thinking clearly. Confusion is the byproduct of disorganization. Peace and confusion, as they relate to being organized, are like water and oil. They can never be in harmony with each other. And they always are seeking dominance over the other. Peace gives you a sense of knowing that you are capable of coming out of your comfort zone, and confusion causes you to become frustrated and therefore, weary about leaving your comfort zone. So create the environment that is conducive for you to operate effectively in making your dream become reality. If it is going to be, it is up to you.

2. Being organized is a positive representation of you. This gives you the confidence to reach your dream potential. Regardless of how people view you on the outside, they can never take away the potential that exists on the inside. But unfortunately, we live in a society that is consumed with judging a person by her outer appearance, rather than getting to know

the person and recognizing the potential that exists inside. Organization is one of many components that describe your character, and as a result, being organized allows you to exist in an environment that gives you confidence. This challenges you to tap into your potential. Being organized becomes a trademark you develop for yourself, and therefore, you are conveying a message to those around you that you are reliable and well equipped to take on the tasks that have been assigned to you.

There are four reasons why being organized is a positive representation of you:

- It keeps you motivated, therefore producing a positive self-image.
- It keeps you constantly prepared for opportunities.
- It enables you to feel secure knowing you will be able to function effectively and efficiently when situations arise.
- It keeps your thinking pattern stable, and as a result, people are more apt to rely on your decisions.

3. Being organized brings forth new association. You begin to associate with people who support your dream. According to I.V. Hilliard, there are two types of friends you should have in your life: those who push you up where you belong, and those who will pull you up where they are. Both types of friends are influential from the standpoint that they not only understand your dream, but they encourage and mentor you while you are fulfilling your dream.

When you have an organized lifestyle, your circle of influences shifts and may downsize. You begin to become cautious of those with whom you associate because some friends may be dream killers. A dream killer is a person who intentionally or unintentionally suffocates your dream and kills the life that once dwelled within it. Those kinds of friends have got to go. It is important to create a circle of influences that is filled with people who have their own dreams, and either are making them become reality or are already living them. A positive circle of influences creates a healthy social environment that allows you to share thoughts, give advice, get advice and, most importantly, motivate one another to pursue dreams. Les Brown said this about relationships, or circles of influences: "There are two types of relationships, a toxic relationship and a nurturing relationship. A toxic relationship causes an infection in your vision; a nurturing relationship helps develop your vision. A toxic relationship blinds your vision; a nurturing relationship sees your vision. A toxic relationship deports your vision; a nurturing relationship supports your vision. A toxic relationship detests your vision; a nurturing relationship loves your vision." What kind of relationships do you have?

If your friends only talk about doom and gloom, then there is something wrong. You will never feel comfortable sharing your dream with your friends for two reasons. First, your friends may not be able to mentally process your dream. It is not their dream, and you cannot make anyone understand your dream. That is worse than making a child eat liver when you know he hates it. Second, your friends may not be able to perceive your dream at the level you perceive it. Once you have a dream and it drops into your inner man, it becomes a desire. There is a mental transformation that takes place. It will lift you out of your comfort zone. Once this happens, your friends still may be operating at a different level of understanding. So if your friends laugh at you or make sarcastic remarks about your dream, keep your cool and remember this advice:

- It's your dream and no one else's.
- The desire is within you, not anyone else.
- It is not someone else's works, but it is your efforts that will bring the dream to pass.

Once I told someone that one day, I'll have my own talk show, and it will be known all over the world. This person just looked at me like, "Yeah, right!" But that doesn't bother me because I know the potential that exists inside of me. I thought I would give that individual a glimpse of what was going to happen in the future, but this person was not ready for it. This type of person should be labeled a dream killer. It was important that I didn't allow this individual to suffocate the life from my dream. However, I have learned to ignore those who can't see my vision. I encourage you to keep believing because your dream will become reality.

4. Being organized helps you achieve your goals and, ultimately, your dream. An achiever looks beyond his senses when it comes to seeing his dream become reality. What does it mean to

achieve? According to Webster's Dictionary, to achieve means to bring to a successful end or to accomplish some purpose. Then what is an achiever? An achiever is someone who is always led or driven to succeed. This person is obsessed with reaching the goals needed to fulfill the dream.

Have you ever craved a certain type of food and had to have it right away? Nothing else seems to satisfy your taste buds until you have that slice of pizza or ice cream sundae. Sometimes a craving can be so strong that you will drive the distance it takes to fulfill it. This is often true with pregnant women, who sometimes insist their husbands drive high and low to find her desired treat. This kind of craving occurs with dreams. Once your dream transforms into a desire, a craving occurs within your inner man that causes you to yearn for your dream to be birthed into reality. This overwhelming craving causes you to look beyond your senses and even go against the odds, which normally prevent you from seeing your dream become reality.

An achiever acquires such an appetite for that desire that it begins to consume his inner man, causing him to envision himself in the future. You have to see yourself in the future. If it is a teacher that you desire to be, then go into a classroom setting—not just any classroom setting, but the grade you want to teach. Feel the atmosphere, then imagine yourself teaching the class. If you want to take it a little bit further, go to the shopping center and try on clothes that you will be wearing in the future as a teacher. Have a friend take of picture of you in the classroom dressed in your selected attire. Take the picture home and start creating your own private commercial, meditating day and night on the vision. An achiever pushes the dream forth by working outwardly and using the resources that are available in the present to make his dream become reality. Don't rush over that statement. Let it marinate into your inner man. Ask yourself these questions: Have you acquired an appetite for your desire? What measures are you taking to fulfill your craving? How far will you travel to take care of the craving that resulted from your desire?

5. Being organized helps you to be more focused. Being focused is being at a point of concentration that enables you to eliminate anything or anyone that distracts you from fulfilling the dream and possessing the desire. It is important to realize that in the process of being organized, you have to be focused. Where so

many people miss the mark is they are unable to focus on what it would take to accomplish the goals that are associated with their dream. Your surroundings—people, places and things—must line up with your dream before you can clearly establish and obtain goals that are centered around your dream. Imagine your dream contained within a perfect circle, which represents a productive environment. You have the power of maintaining that perfect circle for your dream to be safe and untampered with. Now imagine a side-tracker tries to come in and disturb the perfect circle by distorting its shape, therefore, decreasing the productivity within your environment.

What are side-trackers? They include negative friends, a preoccupation with soaps, unproductive talk shows, events that are not beneficial to your dream (such as partying all the time), family members and friends always wanting you to help them fulfill their dreams but never acknowledging yours, a negative attitude towards life and self, and gossip. You probably could make a list of side-trackers that you have encountered.

What is the purpose of side-trackers? To put it simply, it is to keep you from being focused by consuming your time, thoughts and energy needed to invest in your dream so it becomes reality. During my freshman year in college, I always would buy my lunch in the cafeteria and sit in front of the television and watch soaps. One day I happened to observe my surroundings. I noticed few people were watching TV. Others were doing something school-related. These students were focused on their dream. From that point on, I had made a quality decision to eliminate that side-tracker. It was consuming my thoughts and time, and, most importantly, it was disturbing the circle, the productive environment in which my dream was being contained.

Once while I was teaching a seminar on organization and talking about side-trackers, a woman said her big side-tracker in life was her attitude. She said she was so critical about everything that she had done in life that it prevented her from pursuing her dreams. What are your side-trackers?

6. Being organized creates time awareness. Respect time, and time will respect you. Time is one of the most important concepts in this chapter. It is crucial that you as a dream-fulfiller understand not only how time operates, but also how time can effectively

work on your behalf. So many people disrespect time to the point that their lives are stagnant, and as a result, they are either frustrated because their dreams have not become reality, or they have given up all hope and can never envision their dreams becoming reality. In either case, it is the individual's inability or lack of enthusiasm to create a structural setting from which he or she can operate on a daily basis. Time is a dominant entity that you need to understand and respect.

So what do you need to know about time? There are three constant factors about time. The first is time has no timing. Have you ever felt like there were not enough hours in a day to do what you needed to do? Have you ever thought how it would be if you could stop and start time? That sounds nice, but time is a God-given gift that you must work with and not against. Often people say, "I'm working against the clock." You can't work against time because it is constant. One o'clock is one o'clock. You cannot make two o'clock into one o'clock, or vice versa. Each hour dominates a certain portion of the day and has to give up its position once another time of the day needs to dominate. Since time has no timing, it's your responsibility to incorporate your schedule within the domain of time. For example, you may work from 8:00 A.M. to –5:00 P.M. Monday through Friday. After getting home, eating dinner and interacting with your family, you only have three or four hours to work on your dream. That may not seem like a lot, but you have to work with what you have. This may be the dream that is going to get you out of that 8-to-5 job. If you invest three hours each night and eight hours on weekends (four hours each on Saturday and Sunday), you have spent twenty-three hours per week and ninety-two hours per month on your dream. A dream doesn't have to be fulfilled overnight, just as long as it is fulfilled. The race is not given to the swift or the strong, but the one who endures to the end.

The other constant factors that describe time are time waits on no one, and each person operates in a different time frame. Imagine it is nine o'clock in the morning and you are in a classroom setting with fifty students. Everyone present exists in the domain of 9:00 A.M. You and your classmates share the ninth hour of the morning. However, each person operates in a different time frame. A time frame is a designated time that has been distributed for the purpose of fulfilling, reaching and succeeding in the course of life.

You and I operate in different time frames, and we are responsible for what we do in our time frames. If I waste my time, I cannot borrow your time, nor can you borrow mine. Therefore, what I have not done within my time frame can never be recaptured. That particular domain of time was instructed to move forward. You have to respect time because there may have been some vital information, words of encouragement or monetary means that existed within that domain of time that could have been beneficial to your dream becoming reality. Time waits on no one. It is your responsibility to be organized. Organize your thoughts, your goals and your surroundings to be productive in the time frame that has been designated for you.

We live in a competitive society, and as a result, we are innately conditioned to be consumed with what others have, as opposed to where we are going. When you operate productively within your time frame, you are less likely to be envious of others' time frames. For example, you and your friend both desire to play professional basketball. Both of you have been preparing for the big day, but your friend gets a call stating that he has just been drafted by the Los Angeles Lakers. The first thing that might come to your mind is, "Maybe I'm not good enough." And if you are not careful, you will start comparing yourself to your friend. It was that individual's time, simply because he was functioning within his time frame. Don't get discouraged. It just wasn't your time. Continue doing what you're supposed to do and your dream will manifest within your time frame. There is a time and season for everything. So keep on dreaming, keep on working, keep on believing in yourself because your dream will become reality.

How long it will take for you to become organized depends on your willingness to change your attitude, your thought patterns and your motivational drive—all of which are essential elements to your becoming organized and seeing your dreams become reality. Being organized is an ongoing process. You will know you are organized when you are able to achieve your dream, desire or goal with the least amount of stress possible, and when you wouldn't change much about the process if you had to do it all over again.

An important point about organization: You should be organized all the time—not just when it is convenient. Being organized should become a lifestyle that you incorporate into every area of your life.

Recap

1. What is organization? Creating a systematic method that requires you to prioritize the elements in your life to operate in an effective and efficient manner to see your dreams become reality.

2. Why do I need to be organized?

   Six reasons:

   a) Organization brings peace.
      - A sense of peace allows you to work in harmony with yourself to fulfill your dream.
      - Confusion is the byproduct of disorganization.

   b) Being organized is a positive representation of you.
      Four reasons:
      - It keeps you motivated, therefore producing a positive self-image.
      - It keeps you constantly prepared for opportunities.
      - It enables you to feel secure knowing you will be able to function effectively when situations arise.
      - It allows you to have a stable thinking pattern.

   c) Being organized brings forth new associations.
      - You need two types of friends: friends who push you up where you belong, and friends who will pull you up to where they are. Both of them understand your vision and are there either to encourage or mentor you in fulfilling your dream.
      - Do you have toxic or nurturing relationships?
      - Stay away from "dream-killers." They suffocate the life that exists in your dream.

   d) Being organized helps you achieve your goals and dream.
      - An achiever is someone who is always led or driven to succeed, and is obsessed with reaching the goals needed to fulfill the dream.
      - An achiever has a craving, a desire that exists inside his inner man yearning to come forth into reality.

   e) Being organized helps you to focus.
      - Being focused is being at a point of concentration that enables you to eliminate anything or anyone that dis-

tracts you from fulfilling your dream and possessing your desire.

- Side-trackers consume your time, thoughts and energy you need to invest in your dream so it becomes reality.

f) Being organized creates time awareness.

- Three constant factors describe time: Time has no timing; time waits on no one; each person is given his own time frame.
- Respect time, and time will respect you.

3. How long will it take for me to be organized? It depends on your willingness to shape your attitude, your thought patterns and your motivational drive, all essential in making your dream become reality.

4. How will I know when I am organized? When you are able to obtain your dreams, desires or goals with the least amount of stress.

5. When should I be organized? Right now and always.

A Dreamer's Affirmation for Choosing the Right Friends

I will respect my dream. I take full responsibility for those who come in contact with my dream. I choose to avoid people who intentionally try to suffocate the life out of my dream by their negative comments and/or sarcastic remarks. My circle of influences will consist of people who are capable and willing to speak life into my dream. I choose to associate with people who will either push me up or pull me up towards the level where my dream exists in the future.

A Dreamer's Affirmation for Respecting Time

I am a dream-fulfiller who appreciates and respects the essence of time. I will work effectively and efficiently within the domain of time. I will use time wisely and not abuse the time that exists in my time frame. Within my time frame I will be disciplined, diligent, focused and productive. When fulfilling my dream, I will not, compare the timing of others' manifestation with mine. I acknowledge and accept that there is a proper time and procedure for my dream; therefore, I choose to respect time, and in return, time will work for me.

Notes

Notes

3 Putting Criticism in It's Proper Place

The love a mother feels for her baby is so deep that mere words are not sufficient to describe it. The love you have developed for your dream, your baby, has become inexpressible. Your dream has become part of you, and you have become part of your dream. The two have now become inseparable. Being that your dream is such a valued possession, the thought of being criticized while fulfilling your dream can be quite offensive. If criticism is not properly received or addressed, feelings are prone to be put on the line. Criticism can cause regression, stagnation and confusion. While you are in the process of birthing your dream into reality, you must be cognizant that criticism exists and at times is unavoidable. But if it is dealt with in an appropriate manner, it can be a vital tool that will benefit you in the long run. It has been said, "Criticisms are the condiments that flavor your success." Criticism has the ability to strengthen, encourage and direct, but it also has the ability to weaken, discourage and sidetrack. It is important for you as a dream-fulfiller to not only discern the presentation and the content of the criticism, but also to consider the source from which the criticism came before determining if it is applicable towards the fulfillment of your dream. The purpose of this chapter is threefold: 1) to define and explain the purpose of criticism; 2) to assist you in differentiating between constructive criticism and destructive criticism; and 3) to assist you in disciplining your feelings once you have been exposed to criticism.

What is Criticism? Criticism is an outsider's opinion or judgment that is directed towards a person's character, plans, skills and/or potential. To be criticized is to be analyzed by someone who is looking from the outside in, as opposed to being within. As a result, this person's opinion may not be accurate. For example, I pass by a new bakery at the corner. I look through the window at the fresh-baked apple pie. From the outside, the pie looks delicious. But until I go inside and taste it, I can only assume that the pie tastes as good as it looks. My opinion or judgment is only an assumption.

However, when I taste the pie, my opinion becomes valid. This may all sound like a riddle, but the point is this: Criticism is only a person's point of view based on what he observes from the outside, and therefore should never be seen as the determining factor for the fulfillment of your dream. A good principle to keep in mind is criticism analyzes, but it does not finalize. You must PUSH your dream forward.

What Is the Purpose of Criticism?

The purpose of criticism is twofold. First, criticism challenges you to go beyond the norm. A lot of things we do in life are habit forming. Our views, our communication styles and even our spending habits, just to name a few, are determined by the norms, the rules that we either have established ourselves or that have been established by others. Being that we are creatures of habit, many times when someone or something goes against our defined norms, our senses will send up a red flag warning us to make the necessary adjustments to return to normal.

Criticism can be a norm disturber because it suggests that there is something better out there, if there is a willingness to make changes. But our senses become offended and therefore resistant. The information being presented to our thought process contradicts the information that already has been stored in our conscience, our belief system. As a result, criticism is seen as the enemy and must be destroyed before it changes the norm setting that you operate from on a daily basis. For instance, a norm setting I created was being late for work. I was supposed to be there at 8:30 A.M., but I would arrive at 8:40 A.M. I would wake up anywhere between 5 and 5:30 A.M. My morning consisted of praying, getting dressed for work, having breakfast, preparing my lunch, feeding the dogs and cleaning certain areas of the house as needed. Rather than leaving the house before 8:00 A.M., I would leave between 8:05 and 8:10 A.M., rushing out the door and expecting traffic to pull aside so I could be at work at least by 8:40 A.M. After a while, my mind became conditioned to arriving at work late, even though it was stressful and a bad reflection on my professionalism.

The criticism I received was from someone whom I highly respected. This person said, "Sheryl, how can you expect to go to another level if you cannot be efficient where you are?" Wow! I was being challenged to go to another level, and as a result, I began to select my weekly attire over the weekend, and I would prepare my lunch the night before. What a difference. I felt less stress, and I was gaining more respect from my co-workers. Now my senses did not take this change sitting down. There was a lot of resistance. But I dictate my senses; my senses do not dictate me. Criticism that challenges you to become is worth its weight in gold. Remember, PUSH.

The other purpose of criticism is it challenges you to explore and examine yourself. That's a good thing. It allows you to create an inventory list of insecurities, hang-ups and fears that need to be discarded for the sake of fulfilling your dream. When criticism is in its proper place, you are not only open to receiving the insightful wisdom and/or helpful suggestion within the criticism, but you also are willing to put it into practice. Once put into practice, your perception of self begins to change, and you now realize that you are capable of doing, having and becoming whatever you desire. Criticism that is in its proper place will challenge you to take responsibility in developing a durable self-image that can push its way through the obstacle that rises. Criticism that challenges you to explore yourself is the byproduct of someone who not only acknowledges the potential that exists within your inner man, but also knows that you are in need of a little push to get the maximum result of your potential. Remember, PUSH.

Constructive Versus Destructive Criticism

Once you put yourself in a position of going to a higher level in life, you automatically draw attention and become subject to criticism. As a dream-fulfiller, it is your responsibility to discern what is constructive criticism and what is destructive criticism. This is a must because the wrong words can leave a lasting impression.

That is why I do not allow just anyone to critique me. My dream is dependent on me to protect it. Criticism may be unavoidable, but you authorize what will be presented to you and your dream.

These checklists will help you distinguish between constructive and destructive criticism:

A Source of Constructive Criticism...
- Strengthens, encourages and directs you.
- Challenges you to go to the next level.
- Respects your dream and is careful about how the criticism is presented.

- Is firm, but the content contained in the criticism is enriched with knowledge and wisdom.
- Recognizes your faults, but offers a solution.
- Plants a seed for growth.
- Is considerate and knows the right time to critique.
- Helps to build character.
- Is reliable, confident and uplifting.
- Knows from experience and is willing to share failures.
- Initially compliments the work you have done, then critiques.
- Can see your future.
- Criticizes the act, not the person.

A Source of Destructive Criticism...
- Weakens, discourages and sidetracks.
- Tries to keep you at the level where you are.
- Disrespects your dream and cares less about the damage it leaves behind.
- Is harsh, and the content contained in the criticism may be toxic.
- Dwells on your faults and does not offer any solution.
- If permitted, will uproot your dream.
- Is inconsiderate and has no sense of timing.
- Tries to destroy your self-esteem.
- Is unreliable, insecure and discouraging.
- Can not share his experiences because he did not learn from his past.
- Initially degrades the work you have done, then continues to degrade.
- Cannot see your future.
- Criticizes the act and the person.

Discipline Your Feelings When Exposed to Criticism

Feelings are prone to be put on the line when being exposed to criticism. However, it is what you do with your feelings that counts. If you do not properly deal with them, they can become enmeshed with the criticism. This results in regression, stagnation and confusion. If not properly treated, your dream can be aborted. Just as you need to put criticism in its proper place, you must do the same with your feelings. You cannot depend on your feelings to determine the outcome of your dream because they are subject to change. You can be up today and down tomorrow. You can feel nervous one moment and confident the next. You can feel good about a project one moment, then have doubts the next. I don't ask my feelings for advice when it comes to birthing my dream into reality. Instead I depend on what already has been deposited in my inner man to pull out what I need to see my dream fulfilled. (See Chapter 4 about the inner man.) If it were up to my feelings, I would go back to my comfort zone where my feelings feel more safe and secure. I refuse to be dictated by my feelings because I have a baby that is depending on me to push it into reality. I refuse to depend on feelings that cannot see my future but can only see what exists in the present. Repeat after me, "Feelings do not determine the outcome of my dream." To fulfill your dream, you will need some stability for your dream.

The feelings you express on a daily basis are the ones to which you become prisoner. For example, if you always are confessing that you feel sad or depressed, then you are the prisoner of sadness or depression. You may say, "Sheryl, I don't believe that." Well try saying you are sad, every day for a week, and watch what happens. When you are in the position of being criticized, the feelings with which you are most familiar will be the feelings that you use to respond to criticism.

So how do you train, or discipline, your feelings before being exposed to criticism?

I have found these two strategies to be helpful:

1) Create a positive atmosphere for your feelings so they become immune to that atmosphere created and resistant to any information that contradicts what it is used to responding to; 2) Repeat positive words that declare who you are and what you will be. This strategy gauges your feelings to respond to what you believe. For example, I am always declaring that my book will not only be a best-seller, but also that I will be interviewed by Oprah Winfrey. I'm speaking this dream into reality every day. I have trained my feelings to respond accordingly. If a critic comes along and says my book is less likely to become a best-seller for whatever reason, I am not going to get bent out of shape, nor am I going to let my feelings dictate how I should respond to the critique. I have learned to separate the two, the act and me as a person. I have already created a positive atmosphere to which my feelings must conform. Granted, if the content contained in the criticism is helpful and makes my book better, I will make the necessary changes, but I will not let my feelings dictate my actions.

Feelings, given the permission to roam freely, will take you places you may not necessarily want to go. Creating a disciplined mentality does not give your feelings time to attach to criticism. Remember, PUSH!

Recap

1. Criticism has the ability to strengthen, encourage and direct. But it also has the ability to weaken, discourage and sidetrack.

2. What is criticism? An outsider's opinion or judgment that is directed toward and individual's character, plans, skills and/or potential.

3. What is the purpose of criticism?
   - It challenges you to go beyond the norm.
   - It challenges you to explore yourself.

Constructive Versus Destructive Criticism

4. Discerning the type of criticism to be imparted into your life is a must because wrong words can leave a lasting impression.

Strategies for Disciplining Your Feelings

5. Create a positive atmosphere for your feelings.

6. Confess positive words that declare who you are and what you will be.

Thought-provoking Questions

1. What was your response the last time you were criticized?

2. What role has criticism played in the fulfillment of your dream?

A Dreamer's Affirmation for Criticism

I am a dream-fulfiller who not only recognizes the importance of criticism, but also my ability to put criticism in its proper place. Therefore, I will constantly discipline my feelings so they will not become vulnerable to criticism that is not conducive to the fulfillment of my dream. I will birth my dream into reality, so I will put criticism in its proper place.

Notes

Notes

4 Strengthening Your Inner Man for the Journey

lso before birthing your dream into reality, you will need to develop inner strength. It is not uncommon for a person to pay more attention to his physical man than his inner man. A manicure, a pedicure, stylish clothing and the latest hairdo are all common luxuries that edify the physical man, the outer appearance.

But what are you doing to strengthen your inner man, where your talents, gifts, skills and creativity reside? When was the last time you read a book that spoke directly to your inner man? When was the last time you engaged in a conversation that acknowledged and uplifted your inner man? When was the last time you gave your inner man a manicure? Your inner man is just as important as your physical man. After all, it is your inner man that houses your unique abilities that are observed by others through physical actions. Your future is actually stored up in your inner man. I often hear people say, "He has so many gifts bottled up inside of him." They were referring to the inner man of those people.

It is sad to say, but many people have talents and/or gifts that will remain locked up within their inner man, therefore never having the opportunity to be shared with others. That is worse than Pepsi remaining in its bottle and never having the opportunity to quench someone's thirst. Your inner man is specifically designed to nurture and develop your unique abilities in preparation of being presented to reality. If your inner man is properly strengthened for the journey, then the talents and/or gifts that are attached to your specific dream will bring the manifestation you desire.

Before becoming a motivational speaker, I would always dream about traveling around the world and speaking at big conferences. From an early age, I knew I had the gift or the unique ability to encourage people through words. But my gift had to be nurtured and groomed—both my inner man (i.e. listening to tapes) and my physical man (i.e. practicing)—before attaching it to the dream of becoming a motivational speaker.

Dream-fulfillers, strengthening your inner man is a journey, not a trip. A trip is a short-lived experience, while a journey is a continuous adventure. During this journey, you gain wisdom and knowledge. You also will experience disappointments, challenges and victories. Your inner man must be strengthened for the journey because fulfilling a dream is a process. I believe there is always a desire to become, to have and to do; therefore, it is vital that the inner man be fed the nutrients needed to release the unique abilities that will be presented to reality by your physical man.

Nutrients for the inner man:
- Self-improvement tapes and books.
- Positive affirmations on a daily basis.
- Daily meditation into the future.
- Stimulating conversations with other dream-fulfillers.

On the other hand, a weak, underdeveloped, malnourished inner man only will cause you embarrassment. This type of inner man fails to provide a stable foundation, which eliminates its ability to provide the proper channels for your unique abilities to effectively filter through your physical man with confidence. In other words, your physical man is the byproduct of your inner man. A strong inner man makes a strong physical man. Just the same, a weak inner man makes a weak physical man.

These ingredients weaken the inner man:
- Pessimistic conversations.
- Negative confessions.
- Unfruitful books, tapes and/or magazines.

These things hinder the development of the type of character your inner man needs to possess for the journey. The qualities needed are endurance, perseverance, determination, long suffering, courage and commitment. These are called the fruits of a dream-fulfiller. Your fruits are located in your inner man, surrounding your unique abilities. The purpose of the fruit is to produce the temperament needed during the course of fulfilling your dream, and to assist you in fully performing and receiving the maximum results of your unique abilities. Some fruit is more mature, more ripe than others. Therefore, the fruit that is not as ripe is in need of more cultivating so it can serve you properly during the journey.

How do you cultivate the unripe fruit? 1) Keep watering it with words of life until it ripens. For example, rather than saying, "I have no patience," you might say, "I am patient." 2) Act and think in a way that promotes the ripening of the fruit. For instance, be on time, and envision being prompt for work, school and/or social activities.

The Stout Inner Man

An inner man that is fed properly and consistently becomes stout. Stout is defined as bulky or robust in figure; strong, hearty or sturdy body; brave or dauntless. This can serve only as an advantage to the dream-fulfiller. Depositing positive, edifying information into your inner man creates a robust frame that is sturdy enough to not only contain, but release the confidence needed to fulfill your dream. (See the Chapter 18 on confidence.) This inner man becomes the ideal inner being that has been engrafted into your physical man. As a result, your physical man becomes a carbon copy of your inner man.

As I travel on this journey, I have come to the conclusion that I am not alone. There is a special friend that has made a commitment to travel with me on this journey. We have so much in common. We think alike, we talk alike and, most importantly, we dream alike. No, I am not alone on this journey. I have a friend who is not intimidated by the future, but boldly faces the direction that leads to our dream. My friend is like no other friend I ever have had. My friend is filled with wisdom and knowledge and is willing to share to help me make the right decision on my journey. My friend is strong, courageous and firm, and does not give up easily when disappointed or when experiencing challenges. My friend knows how to be patient and maintain a positive composure because being defeated is not an option.

I am not alone on the journey. I have a best friend guiding me to where my dream resides. I would like to introduce you to my friend—my inner man.

Recap

1. The inner man is specifically designed to nurture and develop your unique abilities in preparation of being presented to reality.

2. The inner man must be properly fed the nutrients needed to release the unique abilities that will be presented to reality through your physical man.

3. The fruits of a dream-fulfiller: endurance, perseverance, determination, long suffering, courage, and commitment.

Thought-provoking Questions

1. Are you feeding your inner man the right nutrients?

2. What nutrients are you feeding your inner man?

3. Do you possess all the fruits of the dream-fulfiller? If not, which ones do you need to cultivate in your life?

A Dreamer's Affirmation For the Inner Man

I choose to deposit words of life into my inner man, for it is my inner man that contains the words that determine my destiny. My inner man is implanted and rooted with words that have the power to keep my mind in line and in agreement with my dream.

Notes

Notes

5 Having the Attitude of Expectancy

As you nurture your unique abilities, you must develop the proper attitude. Have you ever heard the saying, "Your attitude determines your altitude." Well, during the dream-fulfillment process, having the right attitude means everything, especially when you are trying to excel to another level in life. It is the attitude you exhibit throughout the process that determines the level of success you will have in obtaining the manifestation of your dream. Each dream-fulfiller should desire to have an attitude of expectancy. This type of attitude always will assist you in maintaining control of your feelings and/or emotions when faced with negative thoughts, comments and situations that contradict what you hold to be true about the outcome of your dream.

What is an attitude of expectancy? It is being able with patience and composure to look beyond what you can see, while waiting to receive what you cannot see. An attitude of expectancy is putting a demand on the invisible realm to release what rightfully belongs to you. You can expect something when you know you have a right to have it. An attitude of expectancy is putting a demand on yourself to do what you need to do in the visible realm to prepare for the manifestation of your dream. If you don't expect anything, most likely, you will not receive anything. But when you know you can go from renting a one bedroom apartment to owning your own home, when you know you can go from being employed to being self-employed, when you know you can go from being in debt to being debt free, you have acquired an attitude of expectancy. And with this attitude, it is essential for you to leave the front door, your mailbox, even the kitchen window open because you are expecting something to come your way. Your neck is stretched out like that of an ostrich while you are looking for a package with your name on it. Your antenna is up because you do not want to miss any signals regarding the arrival of your dream. You are on high alert.

Following are the criteria for an attitude of expectancy:

Joy. I often wonder why many people look so serious when fulfilling their dreams. It is as if a solemn expression guarantees faster results. On the contrary, a hard, disgruntled demeanor will not expedite the manifestation of your dream. Instead it will harden your attitude toward the dream-fulfillment process, causing you (the dream-fulfiller) to view the process as a chore, as opposed to a lifestyle.

It is obtaining and maintaining a joyful spirit that sustains, comforts, strengthens and reassures a dream-fulfiller that he is on the brink of receiving his desired manifestation. Being joyful as if you already have the manifestation (the house, the car, the promotion, etc.) puts you in the position that you have the manifestation. In other words, you are getting a taste of what is to come. Being joyful is not optional. You have to be joyful before you receive the physical manifestation of your dream. Anyway, since you have to wait, you might as well be joyful. It makes the wait much easier.

How do you act joyful? That's simple. First you make up your mind that this is what you are going to do. Then just do it! Be joyful. Start smiling, laughing, leaping for joy, skipping if you have to. All of those physical actions represent the joy that comes from within. I make it a habit to smile and leap for joy every morning because I know it will not be long before I have the natural manifestation of my dream. I am expecting its arrival, so my attitude has to be right. I consider it joy when I face obstacles during the process, for it is the joy that I have that sustains me during challenges, comforts me when I am disappointed, strengthens me while I wait, and reassures me that my dream does exist and is on its way.

So put this book down for a moment and leap for joy or laugh. Don't be concerned if people look at you differently—it is your push that is going to bring your dream into reality. Words of wisdom: You are too far in the game (dream-fulfillment process) to care about what people think or say.

Persuasion. The second criteria for an attitude of expectancy is being persuaded. When you are persuaded about what you cannot see, you are not moved by what you can see. A dream-fulfiller who is persuaded is set, grounded in what she believes to be true. She has bonded and developed a relationship with the process and is convinced beyond the shadow of doubt that if she works the process, the process will work for her and her dream will become reality.

When you are persuaded, any opposition that surfaces during the process is not strong enough to separate you from the process. A dream-fulfiller who is convinced is a dream-fulfiller who is determined. Persuasion comes from the faith the dream-fulfiller has in the process because it has proved itself faithful.

There are three types of persuasion. In the first type, you are persuaded by what you have heard. This is when your thought process is continually being exposed to information that has the ability to transform your belief system, causing your decisions and actions to be the byproduct of the suggestions and/or instructions you have heard over and over again and have accepted as being true. Infomercials are best known for persuading their audiences through repetitious information. Personal testimonies from consumers and convincing "clean-ups" throughout the commercials are being soaked into the viewer's belief system. Before you know it, you are on the phone reading your credit card number. You have been persuaded by what you heard.

The second type of persuasion is being persuaded based on what you know. This type stems from personal experience in past or present events. Information stored in your belief system serves as a reference point and is accessed every time you are put into a position to respond to situations and/or make decisions based on what you perceive to be true. The outcome of each response or decision, either voluntarily or involuntarily, justifies your belief system. Therefore, your level of persuasion increases. Say you bought an item seen in an infomercial. You were persuaded by what you heard, but after trying the product and experiencing the positive results for yourself, you were persuaded by personal knowledge.

The third type of persuasion is based on what you say and is called persuasiveness of the lips. It is a combination of what you have heard and what you know that creates persuasion of the lips. This type is a continual declaration reaffirming what you believe, either positive or negative. In this type, the words coming from your mouth take precedence. Why? You are with you 24-7, and the main voice you hear throughout the day is yours. A creditable source could speak over your life saying you are going to be rich, and that would be a valid statement. But until I start speaking prosperity myself, persuasion is questionable. I am more prone to believe my own voice before I believe someone else's. Therefore, persuasiveness of the lips is wisely instructing my mouth to speak what I am convinced is true—I am persuaded, therefore I speak.

Commitment. The third criteria needed for an attitude of expectancy is commitment. Commitment is the driver of your attitude. It sets your attitude in cruise control so your disposition remains consistent while waiting for the manifestation of your dream.

There are two levels of commitment: commitment out of need and commitment out of want. Commitment out of need is being devoted for the sole purpose of meeting personal needs to maintain existing lifestyles. Personal needs may include housing or transportation. It is the demand placed on meeting the need that obligates a person to be committed. For example, a person goes to work every day primarily to pay bills and to maintain living necessities. Someone who is constantly confined in operating from this level of commitment eventually will become complacent, frustrated or burnt out because there is no other outlet available to channel his time and energy. Someone who always finds himself having to work, as opposed to wanting to work, is in bondage.

Commitment out of want is a self-motivated devotion stimulating a want or a deep desire that is non-existing in the visible realm. The inner desire to possess something makes being committed a passion.

Commitment out of need sets boundaries, whereas commitment out of want goes beyond measures. Commitment out of need dictates to, whereas commitment out of want is directed by. Commitment out of need sustains, whereas commitment out of want fulfills. To what are you committed, your needs or your wants?

Calmness. The last criteria for an attitude of expectancy is remaining calm or settled. I'm sure you have been told at one time or another, "Be anxious for nothing." I know I have. But how can you not be anxious, especially when something exciting is about to happen? It would seem as though being anxious is the thing to do while waiting for your dream to become reality.

On the contrary, anxiety causes a disturbance in your attitude. It fluctuates your feelings and/or emotions as if you were on a roller-coaster ride. One moment you are confident that you are on the right track and your dream is about to manifest itself into reality, and the next moment you are uncertain, and therefore questioning the validity of your dream. Sometimes up and sometimes down, sometimes level to the ground. A person who is not settled, calm or at rest while waiting for the natural manifestation of her dream forfeits her position gained during the dream-fulfillment process. This is because anxiety is like a virus and spreads to a person's thoughts, actions and words. If a person succumbs to anxiety, it can cause her to think unclearly, act irrationally and speak negatively. As a result, the person (dream-fulfiller) has violated the laws of the invisible realm, which can nullify or delay her natural manifestation.

Anxiety is like a thief who tries to steal your confidence. When your confidence has been stolen, you are no longer convinced about what you can have. However, when you are settled, you are stable and you are not going to let a thief come in and take anything that rightfully belongs to you. Think about it. You are not going to let a thief waltz into your office and steal your promotion. You are not going to let a thief come in and steal your clothing store.

Just the same, when you feel anxiety trying to come upon you, you have to resist it by arresting it right away. Read anxiety its rights: "I refuse to be agitated and disturbed. I will not allow myself to be intimidated, fearful, cowardly or unsettled." Tell anxiety, "You've got to get out of this house (your life) right now." Remember, the power is inside you. So open your mouth and start talking. A dream-fulfiller who does not allow himself to become agitated, disturbed, intimidated, cowardly and/or fearful, all of which are symptoms of anxiety, is a dream-fulfiller who is settled in what he knows and is capable of having. A dream-fulfiller who is settled is securely fastened for the drive that leads to the manifestation of his dream.

Recap

1. It is the attitude you exhibit through the process that determines the level of success you will have in obtaining the manifestation of your dream.

2. What does it mean to have an attitude of expectancy? It means with patience and composure, being able to look beyond what you can see while waiting to receive what you cannot see.

3. The criteria for an attitude of expectancy:
   a) Joy
   b) Persuasion
   c) Commitment
   d) Calmness

Thought-provoking Questions

1. Do you have the right attitude to birth your dream into reality?

2. What attitude do you have while waiting for your desired manifestation?

A Dreamer's Affirmation on Having An Attitude Of Expectancy

I choose to have an attitude of expectancy. I have the patience and the composure needed to look beyond what I can see, while waiting for what I cannot see. I choose to be committed. I choose to be settled because I am convinced that the manifestation I am waiting for belongs to me. My attitude determines my altitude; therefore, I choose to have an attitude of expectancy.

Notes

Notes

6 Conception

Now that you know you'll need to be organized, know how to handle criticism, have a strong inner man and have the right attitude, you are ready to take the first step towards birthing your dream into reality—the process of conceiving. Conceiving is defined as to form a notion or opinion, or to be pregnant with. Before the birthing process can be implemented in your life, you must first believe that there is a dream that exists on the inside of you ready to be birthed into reality. Once you accept the fact that you are pregnant with a dream that has to come forth, then you will start preparing for the birth of the dream. It's like a mother who has received news from the doctor that she is going to have a baby. She starts making preparations for the baby. The mother acknowledges that she is pregnant, and she and her husband start selecting names, buying baby furniture and decorating the baby's room to create a warm and secure atmosphere for the baby. How does someone who is pregnant with a dream prepare for the dream, the person's baby, before it is birthed into reality? There are five preparation tools you can use to acknowledge you are pregnant with a dream:

1. Write the dream down and analyze the modifications you need to make to see your dream (your baby) become reality.

2. Create a poster filled with pictures (photos or magazine cutouts) that are associated with your dream. Look at the pictures on a daily basis so you can stay in the future, where your dream resides.

3. Invest in your dream by buying books, going to seminars and finding a mentor. These things are needed to keep you encouraged while you are pregnant with your dream.

4. Associate with people who will speak life, not death, into your dream.

5. Research the resources (i.e., finances, positive contacts, etc.) that are available to assist you in birthing your dream into reality.

The nine signs that you are pregnant with a dream are:

1. The dream is constantly on your mind.

2. You find yourself more in the future, as opposed to the present.

3. You find yourself wanting to spend the majority of your time either doing research related to your dream or working toward fulfilling your dream.

4. There is a level of excitement inside of you that you cannot explain.

5. You take on a dogmatic attitude that causes you to bite into your dream and not to let go until it has manifested into reality.

6. Your inner man is so consumed with the dream that the dream is fighting to get out.

7. You have a new outlook on life. You are able to handle the challenges you may encounter at work, home or elsewhere because you know there will be a better day.

8. You are careful who you share your dream with and seek those who have your best interest at heart.

9. You are not ashamed of the fact that you are pregnant with your dream, and you carry the dream within your inner man with pride.

Recap

1. Conceiving is defined as to form a notion or opinion, or to be pregnant with.

2. Before the birthing process can be implemented in your life, you must first believe that there is a dream that exists on the inside of you ready to be birthed into reality.

3. Five preparation tools you can use to acknowledge you are pregnant with a dream:

   • Write the dream down and analyze the modifications you need to make to see your dream become reality.
   • Create a poster filled with pictures related to your dream.
   • Invest in your dream by buying books, going to seminars and/or finding a mentor.
   • Associate with people that will speak life into your dream.
   • Research the resources available to assist you in birthing your dream into reality.

Thought-provoking Questions

1. How do you know you are pregnant with a dream? What symptoms are evident in your life?

2. How are you preparing for your dream before it is birthed into reality?

Dreamer's Affirmation Regarding Being Pregnant With a Dream

I am pregnant with being/having_____(say your dream), and I promise myself and my dream that I will protect, nurture and love my dream at all times. I will speak life into my dream every day. I will make the preparations needed to cultivate my dream into becoming reality.

Notes

Notes

7 The First Trimester: Learning Who You Are

Henry Ford once said, "If you think you can, or if you think you can't, either way you are right." What a statement! Oftentimes as a greeting I leave a message on my answering machine that says, "The outcome of your day depends on you." Your dream depends on you, too. So many people have not fulfilled their dreams because they have never realized their full potential. They don't really know and appreciate who they are and what they're capable of doing. You may say, "What do you mean they don't know who they are?" If you fail to cultivate yourself, you will lack the understanding of yourself. As a result, you will never become aware of your potential. In other words, knowing who you are defines who you will be. If I ask you right now who you are, automatically, you would say something like, "I'm so-in-so, and my parents are Mr. and Mrs...." That is not who you are. That is surface stuff. When I ask, "Who are you?" I want to know what is down on the inside of you, what makes you tick. A better way to put it is, "What makes you who you are?" Good question. Find some quiet time and sit down and really analyze yourself to see if you really know who you are. I'm not just Sheryl, I am wonderfully and skillfully made. I am creative. I am a winner and not a quitter. I am unique and whole. That is what I mean by knowing who you are. Understanding myself did not happen overnight, and it is an ongoing process. But my understanding and appreciating myself allows me not only to tap into my inner man, but to explore the potential that exists within my inner man.

So how do you learn about yourself? Here are three tips you can use to learn about yourself:

1. Write down things people have said about you either during your childhood or adulthood. If the statements made about you do not match up with what you want to become, make a decision right away to get rid of them.

2. Discipline yourself by spending quality time alone, maybe going to the movies or going for a walk. Find quality time for yourself so you can learn what you like and dislike, what you are and are not capable of doing without the input of others.

3. Observe and learn from those who have a self-image that you admire.

Knowing who you are determines the success of your dream. You should never limit yourself from having the best and doing the best as it relates to fulfilling your dream. Your dream depends on you and no one else. It is your baby. If you have a poor self-image, then your dream will suffer. There is nothing worse than an insecure parent raising a child. Insecurities can be passed on to the next generation. What are you passing on to your dream—a poor self-image or a positive self-image? Remember, "If you think you can, or if you think you can't, either way you are right."

Recap

1. Understanding and appreciating yourself allows you to not only tap into your inner man, but to explore the potential that exists within your inner man.

2. Three tips you can use to learn about yourself:
   - Write down things people have said about you either during your childhood or adulthood.
   - Discipline yourself by spending quality time alone.
   - Observe and learn from those who have an admirable self-image.
3. Knowing who you are determines the success of your dream. You should never limit yourself from having the best and doing the best as it relates to fulfilling your dream.

Thought-provoking Questions

1. Who are you?
2. How do you take time out to explore yourself?
3. What insecurities do you need to overcome to be a good parent to your dream?
4. What dreams have you denied the opportunity to become reality because you did not know who you were?

A Dreamer's Affirmation for Confirming Who You Are

I choose to believe in myself. I am unique, whole and special. I am aware of what I am capable of doing or having because I know and believe in myself. I choose to have confidence in myself because I know that the success of my dream depends on me.

Notes

Notes

8 Creating the Right Image

Do you know that when you take time to learn who you really are, you are going to learn some things about yourself that you do not like? If you were to look in the mirror, would you see something you did not like? Would you consider it to be a habit? If so, have you tried to break this habit? How has this habit helped you to address change? What kind of results have you received as a result of implementing this habit? Does this habit interfere with your being an effective dream-fulfiller?

These are pertinent questions when it comes to learning about yourself, and about accepting yourself during and after change. Dream-fulfillment is all about change and learning about self. I have learned and am still learning from life experience that change brings out things (i.e. attitudes, behavior, beliefs, feelings, emotions, habits, etc.) that you may not necessarily want to come out. It is during these changes or transitions in life that the inner image, the interior self, is exposed and the surface, the exterior self, can no longer cover up the real you. You are left with the choice of making changes to adapt to change, or settling for just being.

For many people, this is a hard decision. People either have created or generationally inherited patterns, or habitual lifestyles to address changes and to rectify self during changes. These patterns or habitual lifestyles may have become deeply rooted, causing people to be resistant to change for the sake of not dealing with self. Many people have become complacent in receiving minimal result, denying themselves the opportunity to get the most out of learning who they really are and what they are capable of having. This is not only unhealthy, but it is unfair to the real person—a person's inner man.

Your inner man possesses an inner image (interior self) that defines and represents the make-up of your inner man. Just like your physical body is covered with clothing to prevent indecent exposure and to protect your body from elements, your inner man is robed by your inner image, which you have created with the words you speak that have been deposited in your inner man. In other words, you are painting an image on the inside of yourself based on words. This image permeates through your physical actions and becomes the likeness of your inner image.

Grab on to this, dream-fulfillers. This is vital information you need to absorb to successfully fulfill your dream. Say what you have deposited in your inner man is positive, uplifting words that denote confidence, strength and integrity. The inner image that covers your inner man is confidence, strength and honesty. This same image now permeates through your physical actions and becomes the likeness, or characteristic, of your inner image.

The change has to occur from the inside out, not from the outside in. This is where a lot of people miss it. They are trying to fix the outside, when all along the inside is where the work is needed. Have you ever seen someone who has lost a lot of weight, but in six months or less they have gained every bit of it back, plus more? This person jumped the gun. Rather than cultivate an image that can properly handle the change, (losing weight) the person executed physical actions that were unstable and dependent upon the old inner image that was out of shape, causing the person's physical appearance to regress to the state in which it started.

This shows that your physical actions can never rise above the level of your inner image. Your physical actions are governed by your inner image. You are what you are attracted to. You may be thinking, Sheryl, I disagree with this statement. There are a lot of people who are successful in life, even though they may be unhappy on the inside. This is true, but you can only wear a mask for so long; the real you eventually will prevail. It is not uncommon for a successful person who seems like he has it all together to end up taking medication for depression, or even to contemplate suicide. The person's physical actions (likeness of their inner image) gravitated to the inner image with which it is most familiar.

Like with many people, including this person, your inner image may be in need of a revival. If you know anything about revival, those who attend come for different reasons. In the case of an inner image revival, someone may need a touch up. Another person's inner image may need a total overhaul. Whatever it may be, an inner image that has been revitalized by being cultivated in good soil (via positive affirmations, speaking words of life, reading uplifting materials) will be able to direct you during the dream-fulfillment process. So how do you create the right inner image?

Have a Desired Result

Before you begin, you should ask yourself what kind of image you desire to have. Remember, the image you create defines and represents your inner image. Your inner man is the real you. You should be sensitive when selecting your inner image because it is your inner man that directly communicates with the invisible realm. The inner image that is built has to present itself as being identical to, or in agreement with, your dream that resides in the invisible realm.

For instance, if your dream is to lose weight, then the image that is created inside of you is that of being slender and fit. However, the same image of being slender and fit cannot be used when your dream is to be prosperous. There is an image for every dream.

Once your inner image is in agreement with your dream, your physical actions become the likeness of your inner image. You then start to speak like, believe in, behave like and receive the image that exists inside of you. This metaphoric experience is what produces the physical manifestation of your dream.

Notice the order, first the dream, then the image that is identical to the dream, then the likeness (physical actions) of the inner image, then dominion. Creating the right inner image is how you can make your dream become reality. So PUSH!

Breaking Habits

Not every habit you develop in life is bad. Greeting people with a smile, brushing your teeth on a regular basis and paying your bills on time are considered good habits. But there are some bad habits that need to be broken, especially when they can interfere with the development of your desired inner image.

What is a habit? A habit is any customary practice or use. Bad habits include negative confessions, inconsistency, laziness, unreliability, procrastination and the tendency to be easily offended, to name a few.

Trying to break a bad habit can be challenging, especially if you have been doing it for a long time. In fact, it can be frustrating when you are making an honest effort to break a habit, then you slip. Slipping is not uncommon, so don't beat yourself up over it and get stuck in the habit again. Instead, get up and get back to work. My motto is, "A habit made is a habit that can be broken."

The diagram below illustrates the journey—including the hurdles—to your target inner image. Point A represents your current inner image. Point B represents the inner image you desire to have. The space between point A and point B is what I call the "in-betweens." The in-betweens not only represent the hurdles (in this case, bad habits) that can make it difficult for you to leave point A and arrive at point B, but the in-betweens also can represent life changes that occur during the dream-fulfillment process. No doubt, things do change (i.e. financially, physically, socially and mentally) when you are pursuing your dreams. The space (in-betweens) should not be conclusively viewed as anything negative, but rather a chance to learn about the real you as well as any modifications needed.

Diagram 1

In-betweens

Point A ------------------   ------------------Point B

  (Current inner image)   Life changes   (Desired inner image)

These three simple principles will help you break a bad habit:

Principle # 1: Acknowledge the habit; be real with yourself. This involves deep soul-searching to reveal which habits have been a hindrance to your progressing in life. When you recognize the existence of your habit and the smoke screen it has created to prevent you from looking beyond the external self, you are on the road to developing the right inner image, which leads to the right destiny. Acknowledging your habits is the first step toward denouncing pride and denial, which both endorse bad habits and leave a person enslaved to an inner image that opposes the unique abilities that exist inside of the person. A habit that is never acknowledged is a habit that is never broken.

Principle # 2: Address the habit; deal with yourself. Once you acknowledge the habit, you are ready to address it by establishing goals and action steps that will put you in the position of being confrontational with the cause, or root, of the habit. For example, a person's habit of complaining may be the byproduct of a family environment where the communication style consisted of complaining. The person's goal would be to reduce the number of times during the day that she complains. An action step would be to have someone else monitor the number of times the person complains.

Principle # 3: Act the opposite of the habit; discipline yourself. This involves being confrontational toward the physical actions associated with the bad habit by implementing new physical actions that are the opposite. This allows you to discipline yourself by establishing a regiment that keeps you on the opposite side of the habit. In other words, you are looking at the habit from the other side, and therefore, you can see yourself leaving point A and heading toward point B.

Paint the Right Image With Your Words

The third step toward creating the right inner image is to paint the right inner image with the words you speak. If you have not figured it out by now, words are the force behind successful dream-fulfillment. Every time you open your mouth, you are creating energy that will either start working for or against you during the course of fulfilling your dream. Words unspoken are useless. Once you speak, you become the artist of your destiny. Kenneth Copeland once said, "Words create an image on the inside of you. Every time you speak words that pertain to your inner image, your inner image becomes stronger until you begin to see yourself as being that image. Once your inner man has conceived this new image, then it permeates through your physical actions."

Sounds simple. What then prevents people from creating the right image? Many people focus on what they cannot do instead of what they can do. "I can't have this." "I'm not good enough." "That house is too expensive for me." "I will always work an eight to five job." The picture they have painted for their lives is small and insignificant. They have painted a grasshopper image, which has caused them to settle for less. It is out of the question for someone who has a grasshopper image to dream about being a doctor, a lawyer or a millionaire because these types of dreams are considered giants, and their perception of self is smaller than the dream. Will a grasshopper fight a giant?

Dream-fulfillers, words are what shape your inner image. I once heard a speaker say, "Words are connected to your life." Words filled with negativity create an image that is destined for failure. A wrong inner image sets boundaries on your thought process, physical actions and vocabulary. However, words filled with life and meaning will create an image that is destined for success. These words paint a picture of your dream in your mind and convince your mind (thought process) that this is how things should be.

Recap

1. How to create the right image:

> Have a desired result.
> Break bad habits.
> Paint the right image with your words.

2. Three simple principles to help you break a bad habit:

> Principle #1: Acknowledge the habit; be real with yourself.
> Principle #2: Address the habit; deal with yourself.
> Principle #3: Act opposite of the habit; discipline yourself.

Thought-provoking Questions

1. What image are you painting with your words?

2. Does your inner image match the dream you desire to see fulfilled?

3. What habits do you have that are preventing you from leaving your old image and arriving at your new image?

A Dreamers' Affirmation On the Inner Image

I will speak only the words that have the ability to paint the inner image I need on the inside of me to obtain the dream I desire to see manifest into reality. My inner image is in harmony with my dream, and my physical actions are in harmony with my inner image; therefore, I have dominion.

Notes

Notes

9 The Second Trimester: Reprogramming Your Mind

You will never know what is upstairs if your mind is always downstairs. Have you ever been around people who have a downstairs mentality? They are always complaining about what they can't do or what they can't have because their thought process has been limited. If you introduced something new to a person with a limited mindset, oftentimes he either will get offended or laugh at you for presenting such a thing. These types of people suffer from an incapacitated mentality. This is a mentality that has never been trained to go beyond the norm. Any information that contradicts the information that exists in the conscience, the value system automatically rejects and views as being impossible to accomplish. It is important to reprogram or discipline your mind to think beyond the impossible because your dreams are a vision of you in the future.

Your thought process is the byproduct of two factors: your environment and your past experiences.

Your Environment

This is what shaped the beginning of your thought process. The information received from family members, friends, teachers and pastors helped shape your value and belief system, your conscience. The decisions you make in life stem from what you were taught or what you observed during your early stages of life. So if your environment always consisted of negative talk, sarcastic comments and feelings of defeat, the information that has been stored in your belief system is negative. And this is what you use to respond in life. That is why parents need to be careful what they do and say around their children.

They absorb everything, and it will have a profound impact on them later in life.

Past Experiences

There is always a lesson to be learned from past experiences. Hopefully, the lesson will prevent you from making the same mistake again. Many times past experiences can mentally imprison a person's thought process because he focuses more on the failure than the lesson to be learned from the experience. How? The subconscious automatically steps in and replays (in the mind) "the old past experiences video" that addresses failures. The subconscious plays this video each time you are challenged to come out of your comfort zone. It is the responsibility of the subconscious to keep you from leaving your comfort zone; therefore causing you to handle failures the same old way—focusing on the failure, rather than learning from the experience.

Before you reprogram your mind to get away from these negative thoughts, you need to be aware that it will not happen overnight. So don't get frustrated. A lot of unnecessary information has been built up in your conscience over the years. It will take time to replace the old values with new values that will shape your thought process and produce positive images.

Reprogramming your mind makes your thoughts clearer, more organized, as opposed to being unraveled. It also allows you to focus on how to effectively implement the outer works needed to make your dream become reality. Then you can use the canvas of your imagination to visit your dream regularly and take a glimpse of what is in store for you.

How To Reprogram Your Mind

1) Constantly expose your thoughts to people, places and things that are centered around your dream. For example, if you desire to become a famous recording artist, you should surround yourself with a certain type of music, musicians, singers and concerts—all of which deposits into your thought process and strengthens your dream into becoming a reality.

2) Speak life to yourself when your thoughts contradict what you are trying to believe. I really have to work on this on a daily basis. Negative or defeated thoughts will try to creep into my mind and distort what I believe. I will not settle for that because the manifestation of my dream does not depend on what I am thinking.

I have to constantly remind myself that I will dictate my thoughts, my thoughts will not dictate me. Will you dictate your thoughts, or will your thoughts dictate you? The choice is yours. You must control your thoughts on a regular basis.

3) Feed your mind the right information. There is nothing worse than feeding your mind junk, causing your dream to drown in a pool of negative, nonproductive thoughts. Information being fed into your thought process must coincide with the dream before it can drop into your inner man and become reality. When your mind is being fed the proper information, it not only absorbs, but it also releases the nutrients needed to nurture and develop your dream.

Recap

1. Incapacitated mentality—a restricted mentality that has never been trained to go beyond the norm.

2. Your thought process is the byproduct of two factors: your environment and your past experiences.

3. The purpose of reprogramming your mind:
   - It causes your thoughts to be more organized.
   - Through the canvas of your imagination, you can get a glimpse of yourself in the future.

4. Discipline your mind by:
   - Constantly exposing your thought process to people, places and things that are centered around your dream.
   - Speaking to yourself when your thoughts contradict what you are trying to believe.
   - Feeding your mind the right information.

Thought-provoking Questions

1. What values and/or beliefs have prevented you from going beyond the norm?

2. How do you control negative, defeated thoughts that contradict what you believe about your dream?

3. What do you expose your mind to on a regular basis?

4. Is your dream safe with your thoughts, or is it drowning in doubt and defeat?

Dreamer's Affirmation for Reprogramming Your Mind

I choose to reprogram my mind on a daily basis. I will expose my thought process to people, places and things that are beneficial to the fulfillment of my dream. Whatever is positive, I will think on it. Whatever is productive, I will think on it. I will dictate my thoughts and not let my thoughts dictate me. My dream will not drown in negative, defeated thoughts, but it will swim in thoughts that line up with my dream. I will always know what is upstairs because I refuse to let my mind be downstairs.

Notes

Notes

10 The Third Trimester: Speaking Life Into Your Dream

Victory and defeat are in the power of the tongue. If you are going to make it in life, you must open your mouth and speak forth what you need or want out of life. A person who lives a life of silence will receive the bare minimum of what life has to offer. Words are so powerful that they can build you up or tear you down in a matter of moments. Imagine how many words the average person speaks each day. How many of those do you think produce life? Think about it. Throughout the day, people make defeating statements without even being aware of it. "I'll never make it, I'm broke." "I'll never have that." "I can't imagine being in that position." "I doubt it." If a person continues to speak like that, he will never be able to reach his potential. Henry Ford's famous quote in Chapter 7 states, "If you think you can, or if you think you can't, either way you are right." You must not only change the way you speak to yourself, but also what you say aloud. You must speak life into your dream until it becomes reality.

There are two reasons for speaking life into your dream. First, it changes your views on life. What have negative words done for you lately? How do they contribute to your dream becoming reality? You may say, "It helps me to face reality just in case my dream doesn't come true," or, "I don't like to get my hopes up too high. Something may go wrong." Those are poor excuses. The truth is, you cannot perceive what exists in your future, or you feel uncomfortable being in the unknown. You cannot straddle the fence when it comes to fulfilling your dream. Either you believe in your dream, or you don't.

Either you believe in yourself, or you don't. You will be amazed at how you will begin to see the world from a whole different perspective when you start speaking life into your dream. SO SPEAK LIFE!

Positive words create an atmosphere that allows you to move freely while working toward fulfilling your dream. Negative words create an in-the-box mentality, which keeps you cramped up, unable to move forward or backward. Speaking life into your dream makes you realize you don't have to settle for what life presents to you, but you can take the resources around you and make them work on your behalf. So if life gives you lemons, take the lemons and make lemonade. Then sell the lemonade and use the profit towards your dream. Think about the last time you tried to fulfill a dream. What where your views on life? Did you speak life or defeat? What was the outcome? Were you satisfied with the results?

The second reason for speaking life into your dream is to help you adapt to change and resist disappointments. Pursuing a dream can be challenging and downright frustrating at times. During my childhood, my family loved to travel to different parts of the United States. During summer vacations, my parents would drive to Mississippi to visit our relatives. The roads seemed never-ending and sometimes bumpy. Imagine a bunch of people in a car, traveling over 2,000 miles, never exchanging words. That's miserable.

What allowed my brother and I to overlook the distance and the bumpy roads were our conversations with each other. They made the trip enjoyable.

The road to your dream can seem never-ending. The road may be bumpy sometimes, and there may be unexpected paths you have to take to obtain your dream. There may be times when you experience disappointments and feel miserable. All of these can be symptoms of change, but regardless of the changes you face while pursuing your dream, you must speak life into your dream. Speaking life to your dream causes you to adapt to change and shift into the proper position to continue moving forward in fulfilling your dream.

Changes will come, but it is what you do in the midst of change that determines the success of your dream. "When the task has just begun, never leave it until it's done. Do it big; do it small. Do it well or not at all." —Anonymous

How To Speak Life Into Your Dream

You've heard the saying, "It's not what you say, but how you say it." I disagree. What you say makes a big difference, especially when it comes to fulfilling your dream. The words you speak can either carry victory or defeat, so you must be careful what you say. You ask, "Are you saying I must monitor the words that come out of my mouth every moment of every day?" You got that right. First, you must develop a confession that you can speak over yourself and your dream on a daily basis. Confessions can be a collection of quotes from the Bible, famous quotes, words of encouragement from influential people or a combination of these things. Daily confessions are spoken out loud not only to declare that you believe in yourself and your dream, but also to keep your thoughts constantly lined up with your inner man until your dream becomes reality. You may want to record your confession and play it over and over again throughout the day. If anything will convince you that your dream will become reality, it's your own voice. Speaking life to your dream through daily confessions is not a choice; it's an obligation. By doing this, you are talking as if your dream already exists. In other words, confessions should be stated in present, not future, tense. For example, "I know I am going to be a millionaire" is a future tense confession, but, "I am a millionaire" is a present tense confession.

You ask, "Did you not say our dream lives in the future?" Yes, but you must speak as if you have it now. Hoping and wishing will not help during this journey. You must know that you will become or that you will have before it becomes reality. Speak with boldness and confidence. Speaking without confidence is worse than not speaking at all.

Speaking with boldness and confidence confirms your belief in yourself and your dream. Speak and have, or don't speak and go without.

Putting Pressure on the Words You Speak

If you want to see results, you are going to have to open your mouth and put pressure on the words you speak—not just any words, but words that speak life, moving the process of dream-fulfillment forward. A lot of people are frustrated and about to give up because they are not seeing their dreams become reality. I wonder how often they speak life into their dreams to produce the results they desire. How much pressure are you as a dream-fulfiller putting on the words you speak to push your dream into reality? There are four reasons you should put pressure on the words you speak:

1. **To remove doubt**. By constantly putting pressure on the words you speak (i.e. via affirmation), you remove doubt and keep your

thought process in tune with the manifestation of your dream. For example, a dream-fulfiller's dream may be to own her own clothing store. Doubt tries to creep in and suggest to the dream-fulfiller that her chances of owning a clothing store are slim. Rather than accepting the suggestion of doubt, the dream-ful-filler increases the amount of time in the day during which she declares she believes in and receives the existence of her clothing store. Ongoing confession eliminates doubt and trains the mind to rely on the words you speak. By putting pressure on your words, there will come a time when the words that come out of your mouth have more authority than the doubt introduced to your thought process.

2. **To become determined to see the manifestation of your dream**. By putting pressure on the words you speak, your attitude starts to change. It becomes more forceful and possessive because you have bonded with the reality where your dream resides. You are so consumed with the fact that you have the right to the fulfillment of your dream that your actions, thoughts and yes, your conversations, have shifted from becoming to already being. When you go back to school, you have shifted from becoming to being. When you start your own business, you have shifted from becoming to being. You are determined to press forward by putting pressure on the words you speak, due to the fact that what you cannot physically see is more real than what you can see.

3. **To get to the point of no return**. In the movie Castaway, Tom Hank's character was the sole survivor of a plane crash. He was stranded on an island, where he had to learn how to survive. A day would not go by when he would not dream about returning to civilization to be reunited with the woman he loved. He was determined to get off the island, so he made a raft to set sail on a journey that was unknown to him. During his journey, he was buffeted by storms, gale-force winds, huge waves and relentless rain. Any single one of these circumstances could have taken him off course, but he persevered tenaciously. Then, in the midst of the journey, he realized he was at the point of no return. His choices were to mount the task of one more wave and risk it all, or to turn around and possibly die going back. The key to his survival in my opinion was his ability to put pressure on the words that he spoke over his situation.

Dream-fulfillers, by putting pressure on the words you speak over your dream, you place yourself in a position of no return. In other words, you have stepped too far into the reality where your dreams dwell that going back to your place of origin would be devastating. Ask yourself these questions: What island have you left? What ocean are you facing? And how much pressure are you putting on the words you speak to mount the task of one more wave to reach the shorelines of your dream?

4. **To unite the visible with the invisible realms**. There is nothing magical about fulfilling a dream. Your dream is not going to fall out of the sky and into your lap. There is a process, and you must be willing to apply yourself to get the results you desire. In this case, applying yourself means putting pressure on the words you speak to bring forth the manifestation of your dream. This is necessary because you and your dream exist in two separate realms. You the dream-fulfiller exist and operate from the visible realm. Your physical senses dominate this realm; therefore, it only acknowledges what it can see, touch, taste, smell or hear.

On the other hand, your dream exists and operates within the invisible realm. Your physical senses are not acknowledged in this realm. This invisible realm can only relate to the words, thoughts (via meditating on your dream) and actions that require its existence in the visible realm. By putting pressure on the words you established for your dream (via affirmation/confession), the visible and the invisible realms unite. As a result, a transformation occurs that causes the invisible realm to release the natural manifestation of your dream into the visible realm.

For example, an individual currently lives in a one-bedroom apartment. He always has dreamed of owning his own home. He meditates about living in a new home on a daily basis. In addition, he is saving money, cleaning up his credit if needed and looking at new homes. Physically speaking, he is still living in the one-bedroom apartment. However, by applying himself during the process, which includes putting pressure on the words he speaks (i.e. "I believe I am an owner of a new home"), the visible and the invisible realms have united, transformation has occurred, and he now owns a home.

Putting pressure on the words you speak works. You just have to be willing to do it, and be patient while you are doing it. You can settle for what you already have in the visible realm, or you can talk your way to the invisible realm and get what you deserve. The choice is yours. So PUSH!

Putting pressure on your words (pertaining to your dream) is one of the most challenging task of the dream-fulfiller. It requires a lot of discipline and commitment. Some people start out confessing but soon find it difficult to continue confessing due to problems in their lives and/or becoming weary because they are not seeing results. As a result, they start to focus more on their problems than the manifestation of their dreams.

However, a stubborn dream-fulfiller who knows the importance of digging deep looks beyond the circumstances, looks beyond time, and begins to put even more pressure on the words he speaks to bring his dream into the visible realm.

If you don't put pressure on your words, you will be shaken by any and every circumstance or situation that comes your way. Putting pressure on your words anchors you like a ship. When the waters are rough, the anchor (the words) is set so you will not be moved. Even after the waters settle, you still will be standing, speaking words of life over your dream.

How to Put Pressure on Your Words

Take the confession, affirmation and positive statements you have compiled, and begin repeating them over and over again. Pressure begins when you increase the number of times during the day that you speak forth the words that will bring your dream into existence. And be specific about your dream. There are specific words that you must speak to bring forth the specific dream you desire. You cannot speak off course or in a miss. Remember, your dream only responds to the words that pertain to its existence.

Also, repetition is the key to putting pressure on the words you speak. For example, if you confess over your dream two or three times during the day, you might need to increase that to eight to ten times per day. Why? Remember, the visible realm has to be united with invisible realm before a transformation occurs. The more pressure the better. You say, "Sheryl, I find this hard to believe." Well, every time you dream about a new car or a new home, or desire to become a doctor or a successful entrepreneur, you have entered into the invisible realm without even being aware of it.

So keep believing, and keep acting in conjunction with the words you speak because that is your evidence that your dream is real. Imagine a hot air balloon in the sky is your dream in the distance. The long rope that leads to the balloon represents the spoken words that lead to your dream. Each time you pull in the rope, you are putting pressure on the words you speak to bring forth your dream into reality. So PUSH!

Recap

1. If you're going to make it in life, you need to open your mouth and speak forth what you need or want out of life.

2. What is the purpose of speaking life into your dream?
    - It changes your views on life.
    - It helps you adapt to change and resist disappointment.

3. Positive words create an atmosphere that allows you to move freely during the course of fulfilling your dream.

4. Negative words create an in-the-box mentality, which keeps you cramped and unable to move forward or backward.

5. How do you speak life into your dream?
    - Develop a confession statement.
    - Confess daily over yourself and your dream.
    - Confess openly not in silence.
    - Confess with boldness and confidence.

6. Four reasons you should put pressure on the words you speak:
    a. To remove doubt.
    b. To become determined to see the manifestation of your dream.
    c. To get to the point of no return.
    d. To unite the visible and the invisible realms.

Thought-provoking Questions

1. How do you speak to your dream on a daily basis?

2. Think of a dream that you had in the past. Did you speak life or defeat into that dream? What was the outcome?

3. If you had two containers filled with words, which container would have the most words, the positive or negative container.

4. Are you confident when you confess over yourself and your dream?

5. Are your daily confessions present tense?

6. Are you putting enough pressure on your mouth to produce the results you desire? If not, why not?

7. What has been released in your life as a result of you putting pressure on your mind? Are you pleased with what has been released?

A Dreamer's Affirmation Regarding Speaking Life Into Your Dream

I choose to speak life into my dream. For my dream's sake, I choose to create a positive atmosphere in which it can properly grow and develop. When I face bumpy roads, I choose to speak life. When I face a never-ending road, I choose to speak life. When I feel disappointed, I choose to speak life. When I feel miserable, I choose to speak life. Life and defeat is in the power of the tongue. I choose to speak life.

Notes

Notes

11 Meditation

Remember, there is nothing magical about fulfilling a dream. Your dream will not fall out of the sky and into your lap. It is a process. It takes work, and meditation is part of the job. Yes, meditation! Oftentimes when we hear the word "meditation," we automatically think relaxation or finding oneself. But I want to look at meditation from a different perspective. To meditate is defined as to ponder, to muse over and to reflect. This definition denotes a recurrence of thought or thoughts. I want to look at meditation from the standpoint of seeing things that are not, as though they were. This type of meditation is past tense-focused but requires present tense action. For example, through meditation, you have a successful law firm. You can see your law firm through the eyes of your inner man. That is past tense-focused. The present tense actions that are required are continual affirmation (i.e., "I believe and receive that I own my own law firm," "Whatever I set my hands to will prosper"), attending law school, etc. Past tense meditation allows you the ability to observe what you already are, have and/or are doing before you experience it physically. Remember, you have to see it before you can do it, or have it.

The purpose of past tense meditation is threefold: (1) to be constantly connected with the invisible realm, (2) to get a clear picture, and (3) to discipline the thought process.

Constantly Connecting With The Invisible Realm

It is quite evident that if your dream is tangible, you would no longer have a dream, but a manifestation. On the contrary, there are a lot of dreams out there that are unclaimed. It is not that the own-ers do not want to claim what is rightfully theirs, but they may not know the right route to take to get to where their dream resides.

First of all, your dream always will exist and operate within the invisible realm. Although your dream is a finished product in the invisible realm, it has not manifested itself to your physical senses; therefore, your physical senses cannot support you. An individual in the invisible realm is already a lawyer with a successful law firm. But the physical senses have not witnessed the natural manifestation. Through meditation, you are now allowing yourself to remain con-nected with the invisible realm, in addition to developing an insepa-rable bond with your dream. This should serve as a consolation to the dream-fulfiller for the following reasons: (1) It keeps you encour-aged; (2) it keeps you pressing toward the fulfillment of your dream; (3) it settles you that you are not moved by words of others, and (4) most importantly, it strengthens your faith. If you want to see things that are not, as though they were, then meditate. It is your right to meditate because the invisible realm has something that belongs to you. So go get it!

Getting a Clear Picture

I have heard that in Hollywood, when making movies, it is not uncommon to shoot the ending first. I found it to be an interesting concept to start at the end, then go to the beginning. You would think to complete a task, one would start at the beginning and work his way to the end. Dream-fulfillers, I challenge you to go against the norm and visualize your dream as a movie whose ending already has been completed. Through meditation, this can be done. Each time you engage into the invisible realm, your dream becomes clear, there-fore giving you clarity on how to begin the process and operate with-in the process until you reach the end. Personally speaking, when I have clarity about the ending, I know how to speak, believe and act in accordance to my dream. Most importantly, I know how to pre-pare, form and fashion my environment so that I receive the natural manifestation of my dream.

Disciplining the Thought Process

The third purpose of meditation is to discipline your mind. Your mind can take you places where you may not want to go. A mind that wanders is a mind that is left unsupervised. Meditation keeps your mind from parking in the wrong place and pondering on negative thoughts that have the ability to rip your dream to shreds. It is your duty as a dream-fulfiller to be careful about the things to which you are exposing your mind. I have learned from experience that when I subject my mind to things that are not beneficial to the fulfillment of my dream, I am meditating more on what I need not think about, as opposed to what I should be thinking about, my dream. There is nothing worse than irrelevant stuff taking precedence in your mind and leaving little space for your dream. Through meditation, you are constantly training your mind to think in line with what you desire to see manifested. A mind that is disciplined removes doubt and fear while on the journey of fulfilling your dream.

How to Meditate

Meditation is not a chore, but a vital tool that assists in solidifying the bond between you and your dream. Whether you are aware of it or not, you were innately designed to meditate. Meditation is nothing new; you just have to put it into practice. Meditation is a gift. But it is up to you to receive the gift and to open up the package. Let me assist you in opening up your gift so you can start enjoying what the gift can offer.

Before meditation can begin, you need to ask yourself these two questions: Am I constantly depositing an abundant supply of positive information into my inner man to sustain me when I enter into the invisible realm? How much quiet time have I set aside for meditation? These questions are essential as they challenge you to evaluate your level of commitment for the birth of your dream. When you are confident in the level of commitment you have established for your dream, you are ready to meditate.

The first step in meditation is finding a quiet place (i.e. going for a drive) that blocks out external distractions. Step two: Imagine yourself living out your dream (i.e. recording in the studio, playing professional basketball, etc.). Step three: Implement your personal confessions (affirmations) while meditating on the fulfillment of your dream. For example, your dream may be freedom from debt. In this case, I recommend you meditate on seeing each one of your bills paid off, while at the same time confessing that you are debt free and walking in abundance.

How Long Do You Meditate?

I do not like to put a time limit on meditation, but if you need one, I would recommend at least ten to fifteen minutes, three times a day, especially if you are a first-time dream-fulfiller. However, I am a firm believer that meditation should not have a time limit because one, bonding with your dream is an ongoing process, and two, you should never leave the invisible realm without having the reassurance that your dream will be birthed into reality. Eventually, meditation will become second nature to you. You will find yourself meditating throughout the day. So before you judge meditation, try it. You have nothing to lose, but everything to gain.

What Type of Meditator Are You?

Everyone has the ability to meditate, but everyone does not meditate on the same level. What differentiates a dream-fulfiller who has mastered meditation from one who is still grasping the concept of meditation is the time spent in meditation and the belief that her dream has more validity to her than her present condition. It is not impossible to master meditation, but it takes time, discipline, commitment and patience.

There are three types of meditators: a visitor, a ritualist and a dweller. Each type of meditator is a choice. Each views and operates within the invisible realm at different levels. There is always room for advancement (i.e. visitor to ritualist, or ritualist to dweller), but that is solely based on the dream-fulfiller's level of expectancy and the discipline, commitment and patience she is willing to invest during the dream-fulfillment process.

The Visitor

The visitor is like a daydreamer. This person is constantly going in and out of the invisible realm, but nothing ever materializes from his visit to the invisible realm. And it is questionable if he wants anything to materialize. The visitor never takes the time to develop a true appreciation for meditation, due to the fact that he never took the time to understand the importance of meditation and its impact on the invisible realm. He has little interest in bonding with his dream. As a result, his dream is confined to just a fairy tale. Lastly, a visitor does not recognize meditation as a gift, but rather a place to go to when needed.

The Ritualist

The ritualist is more advanced than the visitor from the standpoint that she not only understands the purpose of mediation, but also knows how to speak fluently the language of the invisible realm to cause the release of her desired manifestation. However, she seldom gets the results she desires because she does not go the extra mile it takes to possess what is rightfully hers. In other words, the ritualist is a lazy dweller. The potential is there, but it is not being used to its fullest. Of course, this is a disadvantage, as there is no true commitment to the dream-fulfillment process, which interferes with the ritualist developing a true appreciation for meditation. What was not learned during the meditation process stunts the level of appreciation for the process.

The Dweller

Being able to operate at this level of meditation does not happen overnight. A lot of time and commitment needs to be put forth constantly to remain in the position of a dweller. As a matter of fact, there was a time when the dweller was a visitor and/or a ritualist, but then made a quality decision to rise above both levels of meditation to maintain an ongoing fellowship with his dream through the invisible realm. Unlike the visitor, who uses meditation as a mental blocker, or the ritualist, who meditates out of ritual practice, the dweller uses meditation to construct his life and future. The dweller not only acknowledges, but also accepts meditation as being an innate gift. It is through this acknowledgement and acceptance that meditation becomes a lifestyle for the dweller.

The dweller is considered a master of meditation because of his consistency in combining meditation with spoken words (i.e. affirmation/confession pertaining to his dream) that produces a blueprint he lives by in accordance with his dream. This blueprint is then used to assist the dweller in lining up his physical actions (i.e. setting goals, implementing action steps, etc.) with his dream that is waiting to be birthed into reality. The dweller operates from both realms (visible and invisible) with no problem, and therefore receives the results he desires.

Recap

1. To meditate is defined as to ponder, to muse over, to reflect.

2. The dream-fulfillment process is past tense-focused but requires present tense action.

3. The purpose of past tense meditation is threefold:
    a) To be constantly connected with the invisible realm.
    b) To get a clear picture.
    c) To discipline the thought process.

4. Steps of meditation:
    a) Find a quiet place.
    b) Imagine yourself living out your dream.
    c) Implement your personal confessions while meditating on the fulfillment of your dream.

5. Three types of meditators:
    a) The visitor, who is like a daydreamer.
    b) The ritualist, who is a lazy dweller.
    c) The dweller, the master of meditation, who uses meditation to construct his life and future.

Thought-provoking Questions

1. What type of meditator are you?

2. If you are not a dweller, what is it going to take for you to become one?

3. How often do you meditate?

4. What do you meditate on?

A Dreamer's Affirmation on Meditation

I will meditate on my dream day and night so that I will prosper, deal wisely, and have good success.

Notes

Notes

12 The Visible Versus the Invisible

You can be a dweller as well, operating from both the visible and invisible realms easily. However, it is hard for some people to accept the fact that they have the same rights as any one else when it comes to their dreams becoming reality. The difference between a person who is consistently receiving manifestation and a person who is struggling with fulfilling just one dream is the person's ability to operate effectively in both the visible and the invisible realms. You cannot work one realm more than the other. There has to be a harmonious mixture between the visible realm and the invisible realm to keep the motion going forward during the dream-fulfillment process. The visible and the invisible realms operate by principles that stimulate the process and produce the results that the dream-fulfiller desires. I believe that if you are open to receiving what I am about to share with you, you will be strolling, rather than struggling. This section goes into more detail about the visible and the invisible realms so you can understand how to effectively operate the dream-fulfillment process.

What is the visible realm? Go outside. Everything you can see, touch, smell, hear or taste is part of the visible realm. The visible realm also is referred to as the natural or physical realm. You do not have to imagine there is a tree outside because it is there. You do not have to imagine that you hear a bird chirping because it is. What you do not have to imagine is the visible.

What are the characteristics of the visible realm?

1. **Time**. Time is an essential component that is employed by phys-

ical beings who inhabit the visible realm. We are conditionally trained at an early age to arrange our schedule around time. Between five and six o'clock is dinner. Get up at six to be at work or school by eight. It is time that we use to assist us in setting limitations on our daily activities. Time is a systematic method that we use to validate our attendance (at work, school, appointments, etc.) and even our productivity.

2. **Language**. The primary language used in the visible realm is the "what is." The "what is" describes people, places, things and circumstances in their actual existence. What is apparent within the visible realm is the proof that it is reality. For example, the statement "I am broke" describes an individual's current condition as being fact. It is a reality that the individual is broke. There is sense realm evidence that confirms the individual's financial position. Granted, the "what is" is not the only language spoken in the visible realm; there also is the "what is to come," but most people are more comfortable with speaking the "what is" because it is more logical.

3. **Physical senses**. The visible realm is governed by the law of our senses (touch, smell, taste, see and hear). Our senses serve as evidence that supports the natural truth of a situation or circumstance that is being experienced by someone and therefore bring clarity to an individual's natural understanding and reasoning. Our physical senses play such an intricate role in the visible realm that our lives and future are shaped by the dictates of our senses.

What is the invisible realm?

What you cannot see, which requires you to use your imagination (via meditation), is considered the invisible realm. The invisible realm is on the other side of what you cannot see. It is located above the visible realm. However, its existence is just as real as the visible realm. You may find that hard to believe, especially when people are constantly criticizing and/or ridiculing its existence.

There have been many comments stating that the invisible realm is merely a fantasyland. But when you do not understand something, it is easy to talk about it. I have found it is difficult for many people to accept the fact that the invisible realm exists for the simple reason that they have mentally accepted natural truths as having the final authority. As a result, these people have set bounds and limitations to constructing their lives beyond the norm.

I challenge you as a dream-fulfiller not to limit yourself to one realm. Regardless of what people say or have said about the invisible realm, it does exist. I don't try to persuade people to believe what I believe. Everyone has a free will to believe what he chooses to believe, and I believe there is an invisible realm that is holding my dream, and my dream is waiting on me to birth it into reality. It does not matter what other people believe. Other people are not going to birth my dream into reality. It is my belief in the process and my ability to work the process that produces the results I desire. So save your energy and don't try to persuade people to believe what you believe. You are going to have opposition; that is to be expected. But remember these things: (1) When people don't believe, that is when you should believe, and (2) it is an inward knowing that supercedes outward conditions. If you are encouraged to continue believing no matter what, you should be aware of the characteristics of the invisible realm:

1. **Time**. Time in the invisible realm is infinite, unbounded, unlimited. Since time in the invisible realm is more advanced, everything is based on completion, whereas time in the visible realm is based on completing. Everything that exists (your career, your own business, your future) already has been manifested on pre-existing time. In other words, your dream was a reality (in the invisible realm) before it became a reality in the visible realm. These are not things that already have been confirmed by sense realm evidence, but rather things that have not manifested in the visible realm. If you always have to have the approval of the senses before something is considered real, you will never receive the impossible. Everything in the visible realm evolved from the invisible realm. Even the visible realm itself evolved from the invisible realm. Before the visible realm was created, there was an image of the visible realm that existed in the invisible realm. After this image was completed (prepared, formed, fashioned), it manifested into its own, separate entity. The visible timing has its own domain, but it (the visible timing) still operates within the domain of the invisible realm. You may ask, "Sheryl, why are you telling me all this?" So the next time you get frustrated and are about to give up because your dream is not manifesting in a timely manner, you will realize invisible timing supercedes visible timing. Earthly timing assists in the process (your physical actions), but it is invisible timing that is already mature and operating in its capacity. Rule of thumb: This information cannot be comprehended by your natural understanding or reasoning, but only by your inner man, which has been specially designed to go beyond your reason and logic and enter into the realm of the invisible.

2. **Words**. Words are what govern the invisible realm. Words existing in the invisible realm are already settled and established, so not any kind of words will do—only words that speak life into the atmosphere of the invisible realm and are in agreement with the words that are already established are the words that produce the desired results for the dream-fulfiller. Words in the invisible realm will not altar for you, but you must adhere to the rules.

Your affirmations not only speak your dream into existence, but while you are waiting for your manifestation, they create a blueprint for you to follow to properly birth your dream into reality. Since the invisible realm operates from pre-existing time, the words (affirmations/confessions) within the statement made would be used in past tense. In the example "I am broke," the words would break all laws in the invisible realm. This statement is a present state of being or condition that the person is experiencing right now. However, when the person takes action and changes his condition, in addition to changing his confession ("I am walking in abundance"), he is now adhering to the laws of the invisible realm and therefore causing the visible and the invisible realms to unite. Words of wisdom, words conceived in the inner man, formed on the tongue, then spoken out of your mouth are words that cause the invisible realm to release your dream into reality. So PUSH!

3. **The inner man**. The third characteristic of the invisible realm is the inner man. Your inner man (see chapter 4) serves as a liaison between the visible and the invisible realms. Enriching words that are deposited into your inner man, then spoken create an image that is a replica of your dream. This image begins to permeate your physical man, and you are now living out your dream. Your dream has to be received first by your inner man before your dream can be a manifestation in your life. Remember, a dream is before it can become. So PUSH!

4. **Belief in your dream**. Believing is the gravy that is poured over the words you speak to your dream. Believing coats your dream-filled words as your dream is released into the invisible realm. This is important to the dream-fulfiller because words spoken must be able to affirm the dream's existence, or it will automatically be rejected from the invisible realm. In other words, your words may be in line with the words that already exist in the invisible realm, but if you do not believe in what you are saying, your words are null and void. Believing is an uncompromising stance a dream-fulfiller must take in

spite of there being no sense realm evidence to support what she believes.

Believing also serves as a connector. It is through believing that the dream-fulfiller is able to connect with pre-existing time and lock into those things that are. This is an advantage to the dream-fulfiller, as boldness comes over her, and she is convinced that her dream does exist, and it is her right to possess her dream and enjoy it to the fullest.

When you are convinced, you are confident. When you are confident, you have no problem yielding to the dream-fulfillment process. When you are confident, you have strength to work the process. When you have strength, you have peace. And when you have peace, you have joy. All these are confirming signs that your dream is about to be birthed into reality. So PUSH!

5. **Receipt of your dream**. The last characteristic of the invisible realm is receiving. Receiving works simultaneously with believing during the dream-fulfillment process. Believing and receiving go hand in hand; one is not effective without the other. If all I do is believe, then it becomes questionable whether I really accept, or if I am ready to possess what belongs to me. Receiving serves as a magnetic force behind the words you release into the invisible realm. This force attracts your dream, then pulls it from pre-existing time into existing time, where it then is exposed to your physical senses. Believing + Receiving = Manifestation.

Recap

1. What is the visible realm? It is referred to as the natural or physical realm. Everything you can see, touch, smell, hear or taste is the visible realm.

2. Characteristics of the visible realm:
   - a) Time
   - b) Language
   - c) Physical senses

3. What is the invisible realm? Located above the visible realm, the invisible realm is everything you cannot see and that requires you to use your imagination.

4. Characteristics of the invisible realm:
   - a) Time
   - b) Words
   - c) The inner man
   - d) Belief in your dream
   - e) Receipt of your dream

Thought-provoking Questions

1. From what realm do you operate the most?

2. Are you getting the results you desire?

A Dreamer's Affirmation the Visible & Invisible Realm

I will consistently receive the manifestation of my dreams because, I know how to effectively operate in both the visible and invisible realm. I choose to speak words that are in line and agreement with the language of the invisible realm, so that I can pull my dream out of pre-existing time into existing time.

Notes

Notes

13 Labor Pains & Delivery

When a baby is ready to come, there's no stopping her. At this point, the baby can no longer dwell in her mother's womb because she has outgrown it. Now she is ready to be exposed to a new environment that will make adjustments for her existence. However, before the baby can come forth, a woman experiences labor pains. They are unavoidable but a sure sign the mother-to-be is about to deliver. You say, "How does this relate to me?" Your dream, your baby, can no longer live in your inner man, which is symbolic of the womb. When your dream has been fed the proper nutrients—establishing your self-esteem, reprogramming your mind, speaking life into your dream and meditation—it becomes mature and ready to be introduced to its new environment.

The labor pains you will experience will be your sign that you are ready to deliver your dream. Keep in mind, all visionaries have labor pains, but each person's tolerance of pain is different. The significance of labor pains is to remind you that this is it, so endure the pain, and the pain eventually will cease.

What labor pains are you experiencing as it relates to birthing your dream? Labor pains can range from being three credits shy of receiving your college degree to being denied that bank loan that would have finalized your project. You may say, "Those sound like complications." Granted, but don't complications cause some level of pain? If labor pains are not properly understood, a person could misinterpret the pain as being a sign for her to give up or may question if the dream is worth pursuing.

Here It Comes, So Push!

Just like the mother-to-be has to push to bring her baby into reality, you, as a dreamer, have to go beyond the discomfort and push your dream, your baby, out of the canal of becoming and into reality. The results begin to manifest when you are able to go beyond the discomfort and focus on the outcome. What is the purpose of pushing? In the case of the mother-to-be, when the doctor instructs her to push, the physical energy she exerts assists the baby through the birth canal.

There are three reasons why you, a dreamer, should push. First, by pushing, you keep your dream from being stuck and suffocating in the canal of becoming. Second, you gain confidence that you can birth again when you become pregnant with another dream.

And third, you will enjoy the benefits of fulfilling your dream, be it spiritually, physically, financially or a combination. So I challenge you to push. When you are three credits from graduating from college, push. When you have been denied that bank loan, push. One bank's "no" is another bank's "yes." If you did not qualify for that particular sporting event, push. Practice makes perfect. If you are an aspiring actor or actress but didn't get that part, push. Whatever your dream may be, push. No matter the degree of pain you may have to endure while fulfilling your dream, push. How will you ever know what you are capable of doing if you don't do it? Imagine how many people have lost the opportunity to benefit from your dream because you were hesitant to release the dream from your inner man.

Patience in the Midst of Pushing

No one ever said birthing your dream into reality would be quick and easy. The fulfillment of a dream is a process that requires you to be patient. What is patience? Patience is an uncompromising ability to wait for a favorable outcome. It is placing yourself in a position where you will not yield or deviate from what you hold to be true until your dream comes true. A dream that is easily obtained has questionable worth. According to Proverbs 21:20, an inheritance that is quickly gained at the beginning will not be favorable in the end. Many people want to become famous, get a new home or become debt-free, but they lack a key ingredient in dream-fulfillment: patience. Some end up with a premature dream that is not ready for reality. Even labor pains sometimes cause a person to become discontent and compromise. This person short-changes himself and doesn't carry his dream full term. When sharp, piercing pain is coming from every direction, patience is the last thing on someone's mind. He just wants relief and will oftentimes settle for a counterfeit, as opposed to the real McCoy. But patience truly is a virtue, and good things come to those who wait. If you, as a dream-fulfiller, can master patience, you will have gained an admirable quality. This quality not only will become part of your character, but also the trademark for your success. A dream-fulfiller who acquires patience is a dream-fulfiller who understands and respects time. (See Chapter 2 on time.) Of course, being patient is easier said than done, but if you will be open to the "why" of being patient, you will not only birth a full-term dream, but in the midst of pushing, you will have become perfected, strengthened, stable and settled. So PUSH!

The "Why" of Being Patient

Why does fulfilling your dream require you to be patient? Why can't it happen now? There are four reasons. The first is dreams have a specific season, a time that has been designated for the dream to manifest into reality. Have you ever heard the saying, "It's his season." This simple phrase denotes that a person is operating appropriately within the domain of time, and the outcome is favorable. Look at T.D. Jakes. Twelve years ago, you probably would have asked, "Who is T.D. Jakes?" But now he is one of the renowned clergymen of the world. I imagine he did not rush to be where he is today, but rather he allowed patience to have its perfect turn. With each push, he groomed himself so he would be prepared to effectively operate within his season.

Look at T.D. Jakes now. Everything he touches is a success. What if he rushed his success by being impatient? He would have been out of place, and his success probably would have been short-lived. The dream that is within its season is a dream that will produce the maximum results for the dream-fulfiller. However, a dream that is birthed into reality before its time is considered a misfit, and therefore will be of no use to the dream-fulfiller.

Another reason you need to be patient when birthing your dream into reality is it produces maturity. Webster's Dictionary defines maturing as coming into full development. Relating to dreams, maturing is arriving at a place where you prepared to be. A couple of examples: departing from renting an apartment and arriving at owning your own home, a place where you prepared to be, or departing from being in debt to arriving at walking in abundance, a place where you prepared to be. When you become mature, you have left behind your attitudes, actions, feelings and emotions that are not conducive to the place where you prepared to be. A dream-fulfiller who exercises patience has come into full development to receive the tangible manifestation of his dream.

A third reason for having patience is it strengthens the next push. While patience is an uncompromising ability to wait for a favorable outcome, wait is defined as holding oneself until arrival or occurrence. What does this mean? Where will you arrive as a result? You are holding yourself until you have fulfilled the goals contained in your current position. Once your current position has been filled, then you are ready to be pushed on to the next position that contains a different set of goals that need to be pursued. Each time you excel to another position, you are one step closer to fulfilling your dream. Each push requires you to be patient. Patience is a holding place that allows you not only to come into full development, but also to acquire the strength and boldness needed to go to the next phase of fulfilling your dream. For each push, force is required. The force ignites you to be pushed to the next position. For example, your dream may be to obtain your bachelor of science degree at a four-year university. Your current position is attending the university. The goals that exist in this position are taking courses that pertain to your major, writing term papers, making class presentations, preparing for exams and, at times, sacrificing social activities that may interfere with your academic performance. Once you have graduated from college, the position has been filled, and you are ready to be pushed to the next position.

What is a push? It is the effort you make to pursue what you want by going beyond the norm. Pushes can be either physical or emotional. You can push your way through school (physical), or you can push your way through disappointments (emotional). You are pushing something so you can be on schedule to deliver your dream at its appointed time. So PUSH!

Finally, patience creates a greater level of appreciation for what you have become. While you are being patient, you are learning how to sacrifice, how to endure and how to overcome so you can be all that your dream needs you to be. When a person has to work for something he wants, his level of appreciation is far greater than when that something is handed to him on a silver platter. He appreciates it more knowing he took part in creating the platter. So PUSH!

Recap

1. Labor pains are unavoidable, but they are a sure sign that you are about to deliver your dream.

2. All visionaries have labor pains, but each person's tolerance of pain is different.

3. The significance of labor pains is to remind you that this is it, so endure the pain, and the pain eventually will cease.

4. If labor pains are not properly understood, a person could misinterpret the pain as being a sign to give up or may question if their dream is worth pursuing.

5. Why should you push?
   - You keep your dream from being stuck and suffocating in the canal of becoming.
   - You gain confidence that you can birth again when you become pregnant with another dream.
   - You will enjoy the benefits of fulfilling your dream.

6. Patience is an uncompromising ability to wait for a favorable outcome.

7. Why must you be patient?
   - Dreams have a specific season.
   - Patience helps you acquire another level of maturity.
   - Patience strengthens the next push.
   - Patience creates a greater appreciation.

Thought-provoking Questions

1. What labor pains are you experiencing?

2. What is your tolerance level for pain?

3. What type of bond do you have with your dream?

4. What messages are you conveying to your dream during delivery? And how does your dream respond?

5. Is your dream stuck in the canal of becoming? And what are you doing to get your dream out of the canal?

A Dreamer's Affirmation for Labor and Delivery

I am ready to push my dream into reality. I have a high tolerance for pain; therefore, I will not be intimidated by the discomfort I am currently experiencing. I will push my dream through the canal of becoming because my dream is destined to be in the land of existence. The time has come, so I must push.

A Dreamer's Affirmation for Patience

I will not be dictated by anxious thoughts or feelings during the course of fulfilling my dream. The manifestation of my dream is the byproduct of patience and perseverance. Patience is a virtue; therefore, I acknowledge that fulfilling my dream is a process. I will not rush the process because there is a level of maturity that I will have gained while fulfilling my dream. I will be patient because good things come to those who wait.

Notes

Notes

14 A Sterile Environment

This section has been written to forewarn you as a dream-ful-filler of what could happen if you do not maintain a sterile environment for your dream once it is born. Say your water has broken, and it is time for your dream to be birthed into reality. All the confessions, action steps and meditation finally have paid off, and it is time for you to be united with your dream. Wouldn't it be terrible if the place (physical surroundings) was not sterile? Could your natural manifestation (the house, the promotion, the best-selling album, the five-year contract with the Los Angeles Lakers) survive? Probably not.

It is healthier for a mother to deliver her baby in a sterile environment. In a sterile environment, the mother and her newborn infant are less likely to be exposed to any form of bacterial infection that could jeopardize their health. The type of environment into which your physical manifestation is born and from which it is operating means everything. Why? Your dream has always dwelled in the invisible realm. While residing there, it was normal for your dream to be protected and nurtured in a positive environment on a continuous basis.

Once the physical manifestation is birthed into its new environment, it has to make adjustments from an environment that is pure by nature to an environment that is pure by choice. If the environment, your physical surroundings, cannot properly assist with these adjustments (by providing the environment your dream is accustomed to), the physical manifestation of your dream will become contaminated and eventually will die. A baby inside her mother's womb for nine months grew accustomed to receiving the proper nutrients and living in a safe environment. However, if the conditions outside the womb are not comparable to those inside the womb, the baby's life span is minimal. For example, if a mother was eating correctly when she was pregnant, but after delivering the baby and going home, she stopped feeding the baby, her baby would die of malnutrition. What a waste!

After birthing their dream into reality, how many athletes, entertainers and CEOs have allowed their dream to become contaminated? The newspaper constantly contains such stories as an entertainer arrested for drug possession, an athlete charged with sexual assault, or a CEO committing suicide because his company went bankrupt—all because their dreams became contaminated.

There are two ways a dream-fulfiller can determine the sterility of his environment. The first way is to detect the bacteria to which his environment is most sensitive. (Note: There can be more than one type of bacteria in a dream-fulfiller's environment.) If a dreamer is not cognizant of the bacteria that exist around his environment, then the cause of death of his manifestation always will be questionable. It is to the advantage of the dream-fulfiller to not only detect, but also learn the make-up of the bacteria so he can properly address it by using a solvent that has been specifically designed to get to the root of the bacterial growth and kill it once and for all.

How can a dream-fulfiller tell if bacteria are lurking around in his environment?

1. **The physical manifestation is slowly deteriorating**. Once the physical manifestation of the dream has been birthed into reality, the dream-fulfiller becomes occupied or down right lazy and ceases to speak life into her physical manifestation. A dream-fulfiller does not stop speaking life just because the manifestation has arrived in her life. If continual affirmation is not applied to the physical manifestation of the dream, the inner image that was created to support the dream-fulfiller during the dream-fulfillment process becomes weak. This interferes with the inner image's effectively permeating the likeness (characteristics/physical actions) the physical man needs to maintain possession of the physical manifestation in his life. For instance, a dream-fulfiller's manifestation has materialized into debt freedom. However, if the dream-fulfiller stops confessing his physical manifestation, his physical actions start to regress back to the old man, the

old ways of doing things (i.e. running up the Visa or MasterCard, etc.). This dream-fulfiller has lost contact with the inner image that has the vital substance the dream-fulfiller needs to stay on track and maintain possession of his physical manifestation in his life. The physical manifestation of your dream is only as good as the image that created it.

2. **The dream-fulfiller is no longer protecting the physical manifestation**. Before the dream became reality, the dream-fulfiller did everything in her power to protect her dream from negative influences. She would not let just anyone say just anything about her dream. Her dream's arrival was going to be a safe one. However, after the birth of the dream, the dream-fulfiller stopped protecting her dream the way she used to and began to let her guard down, leaving the physical manifestation to protect itself. A manifestation such as this that is left unprotected, unattended is subject to negative influences (negative criticism, negative confession, doubt, disbelief, etc.) that come only to steal, kill and destroy the life that is contained in her natural manifestation. Once the life has been depleted from the physical manifestation, it no longer can serve its purpose. As a result, the dream-fulfiller's physical surroundings return to their original state, without form, lifeless and dark.

3. **The effects of the physical manifestation are wearing off**. The excitement of possessing the physical manifestation is not as strong, not as passionate as the first day the dream-fulfiller was physically united with his manifestation. The dream-fulfiller begins to take the physical manifestation for granted, which causes the value of the manifestation to depreciate. When this happens, the dream-fulfiller is apt to have an affair on the physical manifestation, contaminating the relationship. Speaking doubt and unbelief and not depositing words of life into his inner man are a couple of unfaithful behaviors that are displayed by the dream-fulfiller who is having an affair on his manifestation. When the honeymoon is over, the dream-fulfiller moves on to pursue another dream. After a while, the dream-fulfiller is only acting out the dream-fulfillment process, as opposed to living it. He is only deceiving himself because he never fully digested what was to be learned during the process.

There is nothing wrong with pursuing more than one dream, but each dream should be cherished as a prized possession. A dream-fulfiller who has an affair on his physical manifestation is like a man who looks carefully at his natural face in the mirror, but then goes away and promptly forgets what he looks like. Every time a dream-fulfiller allows the effects of his physical manifestation to wear off, he is taking on another identity that opposes the purpose of the dream.

What type of bacteria can be found in a dream-fulfiller's environment? Before a dream-fulfiller starts destroying bacteria, she needs to know what type of bacteria exist in her physical surroundings. Similarly, before a farmer can start applying pesticides to his crops, he must determine the kinds of bugs that are destroying the crops. The farmer depends on his crops to bring forth a harvest, so it is vital that he knows the right pesticide to use on the bugs for it not to be a hit-and-miss situation.

The same principle must be implemented by the dream-fulfiller. He must survey his environment before rushing in with a solvent that may not work. Three types of bacteria are most commonly found in a dream-fulfiller's environment, although other bacteria may exist as well.

Bacteria #1: Nonproductive television shows (including radio shows, certain types of music, etc.). I consider watching television to be the grandfather of bacteria. This type of bacteria has been around for so long that it has developed its own immune system, and therefore has become resistant to many solvents. Television shows have a long history; many people were raised by television. If a person was not properly monitored while watching television, nonproductive seeds were planted into her inner man, producing a negative harvest and creating an inner image that was synthetic, rather than authentic. A dream-fulfiller should be aware of this bacteria, for it is best known for reprogramming the mind and dominating what already has been stored in her belief system. In other words, your thoughts become agreeable with whatever you are watching on television. This is bad news for your physical manifestation because it was words of life and the truth behind those words that have maintained its existence.

Finally, once a dream-fulfiller has fulfilled his dream, he may find out that he has a lot of time on his hands. If this is the case, a dream-fulfiller certainly does not want to fill that time watching nonproductive television shows. My advice to the dream-fulfiller is this: If television is not putting money in your pocket or speaking life into you and your physical manifestation, turn the television off.

Bacteria # 2: Friends, relatives and peers. I am not referring to your friends, relatives or peers as bacteria, but the words that come out of their mouths may carry a bacterial infection. Not all those with whom you associate carry a bacterial infection (words spoken), but you know the friends, relatives and/or peers who have bacterial infection spewing from their mouths, contaminating anything that is positive. A dream-fulfiller who consents to her environment being filled with negative confessions will cause her physical manifestation to become infected. If those friends and loved ones are not dealt with promptly and appropriately, the physical manifestation will suffocate and die. It is the dream-fulfiller's responsibility to avoid compromising conversation that will tempt her to say or hear the wrong things.

I have learned from experience that not everyone can be exposed to my dream, or my physical manifestation. People may not mean any harm, but the words they speak over my dream can be harmful. Therefore, since you can choose your friends and peers, choose those who think, believe and speak like you. You cannot choose your family, but what you can do is stand firm in your beliefs, say very little about what you are doing and let them see the results for themselves. My motto is: The less you say and the more you do, the better off you are. It is just a matter of time before others will see the manifestation of your dream.

Bacteria # 3: The wrong social settings. There are some places where a dream-fulfiller cannot go. Engaging in different social settings (i.e. clubs, dinner parties, movies, cultural events, etc.) is what many of us do to bring balance to our busy schedules, but have you ever been somewhere and unable to fully enjoy what that particular setting had to offer, either positive or negative? I know I have had my share of uneasiness, all brought on by being somewhere I had no business being. I often have wondered why I could not go certain places or do certain things with which other people had no problem. I finally came to the conclusion that a dream exposed to a foreign environment may not be birthed, and a physical manifestation exposed to a foreign environment may die.

As I disciplined myself and began to operate appropriately and effectively in the dream-fulfillment process, I learned that it is not all about going places and doing things, but it is about becoming and giving (becoming a doctor so that I can give back to my community, for example).

Dream-fulfillers, once you have successfully completed the dream-fulfillment process and have obtained your desired manifestation, you have gained a level of maturity that separates your thoughts, speech and physical actions from the mainstream. Your mind has been transformed, and you now look at things from the top, as opposed to from the bottom. During the dream-fulfillment process, your mind was renewed to fashion after and adapt to the principles of the invisible realm. Once you have reached this level, it is important to maintain (via meditation, positive affirmation, depositing enriching words into your inner man) this level so you can discern the foreign bacteria that harbor in a particular social setting.

You may ask, "Sheryl, what harm is there in going out once in a while?" The answer is a lot, if it is not the right place. I can recall from experience, when I successfully completed the process and my physical manifestation was manifested in the form of being cured of tuberculosis peritonitis. I was invited to a social setting that was definitely not conducive to my newly birthed manifestation. Throughout the evening, I heard people complaining about their health—the doctor said this or that about their health. And to top it off, someone said, "I died laughing." My newly born physical manifestation did not need to hear all this negative stuff. Why? Because if I continued to engage in this type of social setting, my mind would have tried to take authority by returning back to the old ideals and attitudes I once had, especially regarding health.

Your mind should never have authority over you; you should always have authority over your mind. And that is done through the words you speak and through meditation about those words being lived out in your life. In that particular social setting, I felt a war going on between my mind and the negative bacteria that existed in this foreign environment. I was fighting to maintain what I believe and not give in to what I used to believe. I don't know about you, but I need my mind to be in sync with my inner man to get the revelation I need for my physical manifestation to occur.

Your inner man is connected with the invisible realm, where your dream resides, and your mind is connected with the visible realm, where your dream does not exist. As your mind becomes more convinced of the reality of your dream and your possession of its reality, the visible realm and the invisible realm unite, and the physical manifestation is birthed into your life.

But if you keep exposing your dream and/or manifestation to foreign environments with foreign bacteria that war against your thought process, this diminishes your revelation, preventing your dream from becoming reality, or taking the life from your existing manifestation.

The second way to determine the sterility of your environment is to eject. To eject is defined as to drive or force out; expel. We want to drive out, force out, expel any and every bacteria that are out to cause harm to our dreams or existing manifestations.

A few solvents are accessible to combat these bacteria that can exist in a dream-fulfiller's environment: **Solvent # 1: Selective television watching**. Watching nonproductive television shows is the grandfather of bacteria, and throughout the years, this bacteria have become resistant to many of the disinfectants (such as stopping television watching cold turkey) that we have used in the past. This type of solvent is able to resemble the bacteria (watching television) in appearance so that the bacteria does not become resistant, while at the same time releasing the chemical contained in the solvent (increasing productive television shows) to wean an individual from nonproductive television shows. This attacks the bacteria from the root slowly, but surely kills it each time it is exposed to productive television watching.

Selective television watching includes television programs that send messages that concur with your inner image. Selective television watching also guides your thought process so that it stays in agreement with your inner image that reflects your dream, or physical manifestation. Keep in mind this solvent does not work over night, but if it is used on a regular basis, your environment no longer will be held in bondage to this bacteria. I recommend that you apply this solvent once a week, then increase that to twice a week and then as often as necessary until this bacteria is completely removed.

Solvent # 2: A positive circle of influence. A positive circle of influence acts as a solvent in that it will not allow bacteria (i.e. negative conversations, negative confessions, etc.) to operate within this circle of influence; therefore, when the negative bacteria surface, through friends, relatives and/or peers, this solvent immediately recognizes the bacteria and kills it upon contact.

Solvent # 3: The ability to discern appropriate social settings. This solvent is used to track down negative bacteria that harbor in a particular social setting. This type of solvent is considered a pre-solvent because it is designed to be used before engaging in a social setting that may be life-threatening to your dream or existing physical manifestation. It is important to ask yourself these questions for the solvent to be effective:

1. Is this particular social setting friendly or safe for my dream or existing manifestation?

2. What will I consciously be focusing on while engaging in this social setting? And if it happens to come across my thought process two years from now, will it benefit my dream or existing manifestation?

3. Will I be easily tempted to act, think and/or speak differently for the sake of blending in with the others who are attending this particular social setting?

4. Will the words exchanged during this particular social setting be offensive to my inner man?

5. Will this social setting cause me to doubt the existence of my dream or ignore my physical manifestation for any length of time?

6. Will I have to get a lot of junk out of my mind after leaving this social setting?

7. How will I benefit from being in this social setting?

Recap

1. Maintain sterility of your environment by:
   Step 1. Detecting the bacteria to which your environment is most sensitive.

2. How can a dream-fulfiller tell if bacteria's are lurking around his/her environment?
   - The physical manifestation is slowly deteriorating.
   - You are no longer protecting the physical manifestation.
   - The effects of the physical manifestation are wearing off.

3. Types of bacteria most commonly found:
   - Bacteria #1: Nonproductive television shows.
   - Bacteria #2: Friends, relatives and peers.
   - Bacteria #3: The wrong social settings.

4. Step 2. Eject, drive out, force out, expel any and every bacteria that are out to cause harm to your dream or existing manifestation.

5. Solvents accessible to kill bacteria:
   Solvent #1: Selective television watching.
   Solvent #2: A positive circle of influence.
   Solvent #3: An ability to discern appropriate social settings.

Thought-provoking Questions

1. How sterile is your environment?

2. What bacteria is your environment most sensitive to?

3. What solvent are you using to destroy the bacteria found in your environment?

4. Can your dream and/or existing manifestation survive in your environment?

A Dreamer's Affirmation on a Sterile Environment

I will not indulge in nonproductive television shows. I highly respect my inner man and the information that is contained within. I will be wise and prudent in selecting the television shows that reinforce the inner image that exists within me.

Notes

Notes

15 The Dream Versus the Trial

This chapter contains personal disclosures that convey the trials I've experienced in life, as well as the strategies I have used to overcome the trials. You might be in the middle of birthing your dream into reality, and a trial unexpectedly comes knocking at your door. What do you do? Do you let it come in and reside in your home? Of course not. You push that trial out of the way and keep on walking. No one is exempt from a trial, but the good thing is no one has to be defeated by one. My desire for you is to master the information in this chapter so you can excel above trials and soar into the future where your dream is waiting.

What is a trial to a dream-fulfiller? It is unwelcome opposition that tries to divert the attention given to fulfilling the dream. Trials can range from an unexpected illness to financial hardship, and everything in between. Characteristics of a trial:

- Can be short- or long-term.
- Targets the most sensitive area of your life (physically, mentally, socially or economically).
- Seeks a person's undivided attention.
- Does not discriminate by age, gender, race or socio-economical status.
- Is the byproduct of circumstances beyond one's control, self-inflicted due to past decisions, or sabotage

The preface mentions that in 1987, I was diagnosed with tuberculosis peritonitis. An unexpected, unwelcome trial had visited my life. It seemed like everything had changed overnight. I had to withdraw

from school. I was admitted into the hospital. My parents were contemplating divorce. Our house was in foreclosure.

It felt like a tornado went through my life and turned everything
upside-down. At that time, I had to decide if I was going to be the
victim or the victor. One of us had to go, and I knew it was not going
to be me. I had places to go, people to see, things to do and dreams
to fulfill. So I had no other choice but to PUSH. I believe the con-
cern of many people, especially dream-fulfillers, is, How do you
defeat a trial that seems bigger than you and your dream, so you can
resume your position of birthing your dream into reality?

Following are four strategies I've used and still use today to overcome trials. First, rehearse who you are before the trial. There is
nothing worse than not knowing who you are when a trial arises. A
person who is uncertain about who he is, what he can do, what he
can have and what he can become always will be defeated by a trial.
It is essential for a dream-fulfiller to declare who he is and what he
will become on a daily basis. For example, I declare that I am the
healthiest woman in the world. There are times when I don't feel that
way, but I do not go by my feelings. When I declare that I am in good
health, I am rehearsing, I am training, I am drilling my inner man,
my mind and my body to line up to the words I speak and not to my
feelings. In other words, I am creating a picture for my mind to use
as a reference point. When a trial comes and presents a picture that
contradicts what already has been painted, my mind automatically
becomes resistant, and my body starts to fight. If I say I am the
healthiest woman in the world, and a trial comes and presents sickness to my body, my mind and body fight the sickness until I return
to health. You may say, "I don't believe that." Well, keep saying you
are sick, keep saying what the doctors say, keep saying that you are
going to die, and see what happens. You have created a picture for
your mind to use as a reference point.

While writing this book, I was experiencing intermittent pains in
my stomach. They became so intense I had to go to the doctor. After
I underwent testing, I was told I had an ovarian cyst. The doctor rec-
ommended surgery and told me it would take a miracle for it to go
away without surgery. I already know who I am. I confess that I am
the healthiest woman in the world. I opted not to have surgery.
Instead I prayed to the same God who healed me of tuberculosis peritonitis. I changed my diet and kept on writing this book. As the
weeks went by, the pain subsided. I went back to the doctor for an

evaluation and had more tests done. The cyst had disappeared. Is this the miracle the doctor was talking about?

When sickness comes, it has no trouble defeating you because it has nothing to oppose it.

Rehearsing before the trial simply puts you in a better position to fight and win, rather than fight and lose. It is always good to rehearse before going on stage. So PUSH!

The second strategy is don't fear when you get bad news. You will find this strategy a challenge to master, especially when people have been conditioned to respond to certain situations based on past experiences and societal influences. Common responses when approached with bad news are worry, fear and rationalization. Emotional and, at times, even logical responses make matters worse because a person is unable to make sound decisions when needed.

When I got the bad news about my health, I didn't fall on the ground and start screaming, but I got myself together and did what I had to do. I had to know who I was and whose I was, and therefore, I could not afford to be in fear because this would have only added extra stress to my body that I definitely did not need. Don't get me wrong, I did not like what was happening to my body, but I knew I had to be steadfast, unmovable in my faith in God and see this thing through. Fear or any other common response only puts up a brick wall that tries to prevent you from looking to see what is in store for you on the other side. When a person becomes afraid as a result of bad news, he is actually telling the trial, "I am scared of you because you are bigger than me." The next time you get bad news, look it right in the eyes and say, "I'm not scared of you. I'm not moved by you. You have got to go." PUSH!

The third strategy is avoid speaking the problem, and speak the solution. Being in the counseling profession, I always hear people talk about their problems as if the problems were celebrities. People can become so consumed with their current condition that the future is unheard of. Constantly speaking about what is does not change the status of the trial. You may say, "Are you telling me to deny the trial(s) that exist in my life?" I am not telling you to deny the trial, but I am telling you to deny that you will be subject to the trial. What if during my experience, I spoke what the doctors said about my condition? What if everyone I talked to said I was sick and probably would not make it? Would it have changed my situation? Yes it would have. I probably wouldn't be writing this book. I'd be pushing daisies.

And after a while, I have learned that people get tired of listening to your problems. I spoke how I wanted things to be. I spoke the solution. Rather than saying I was sick, I would say I am getting better every day, even when it did not look like it. What did I have to lose? What do you have to lose?

Negative words would have only gotten me a quick ticket to the graveyard. At least by speaking life, I was constantly rejuvenating and feeding my inner man, my mind and my body. If a person can speak to a plant or his car, I can speak to my body. By speaking the solution, I dictated the trial, as opposed to the trial dictating me. In other words, the words you speak should always take precedence over the trial. So keep speaking life over you and your circumstances. If you do, even though you don't see life, eventually you will have life. So PUSH!

The fourth strategy is keep the dream alive. When faced with a trial, it's easy to let the dream die. For many people, the trial has become so overwhelming that the energy, time and commitment that was set aside for the dream has been redirected toward the trial. A dream that is not attended to eventually will die. No matter what you are going through, always, always, always keep your dream alive. How? Constantly visualize yourself in the future. Keep your dream board posted in a visible area so you can see your dream. Keep speaking life into your dream. Keep working on your dream, even if it is on a part-time basis. A dream that is always spoken of is a dream that is never forgotten. So PUSH!

Soaring Like an Eagle

Being in the right position means everything if you plan to be on top. When you are on the top, you can see things much clearer. However, getting to the top is where the challenge lies. As a dream-fulfiller, you must envision yourself as an eagle. When an eagle encounters a storm, it has three choices: 1) to sit up in a tree and wonder what it would be like to be on top (an eagle that was not willing to take a risk); 2) fly through the storm and be tossed and turned to and fro and possibly get killed (an eagle without a plan); or 3) ride the wind into high places above the storm (an eagle that is not moved by the storm but uses wisdom while riding the storm).

A dream-fulfiller also has choices: 1) do nothing and be overtaken by the storm, or trial, and wonder what it would be like to be on the top; 2) haphazardly go through the storm by not knowing who you are, walking in fear and speaking what is—which cause you to be tossed and turned by the winds and possibly kill you and your dream; and 3) be prepared before the storm, and when it comes, ride into the high places above the storm where your dream resides.

Those who wait upon the dream shall see it come to pass. That is anticipation. They shall mount up with wings like eagles. That is elevation. They shall run and not get weary. That is acceleration. They shall walk and not faint. That is determination. So PUSH!

Recap

1. Trials should only be stepping stones that lead to your dream.

2. A trial is an unwelcome opposition that tries to divert the attention given to fulfilling the dream.

3. What are the characteristics of a trial?

   • Can be short or long-term.
   • Targets the most sensitive areas of your life.
   • Seeks a person's undivided attention.
   • Does not discriminate by age, gender, race or socio-economic status.

4. What are strategies to overcome trials?

   • Rehearse who you are before the trial comes.
   • Don't fear when you get bad news.
   • Avoid speaking the problem, and speak the solution.
   • Keep the dream alive.

Soaring Like an Eagle

5. A dream-fulfiller's choices when encountering a storm:

   • Do nothing and be unwilling to take risks.
   • Perish without a plan by doing everything wrong.
   • Do not be moved by the storm, but use wisdom when riding the storm.

Thought-provoking Questions

1. How did you respond when you were approached by a trial? What was your initial response?

2. How do you speak when you are going through a trial?

3. What position do you take when you encounter a storm?

4. How do you keep your dream alive when facing a trial?

5. Who will win—you or the trial?

A Dreamer's Affirmation for Overcoming Trials

I am the victor and not the victim of the trial; therefore, I refuse to be subject to what the trial presents to me. I will only speak the solution, not the problem. I am a dream-fulfiller who will ride above the storm. I will soar in high places where my dream resides.

Notes

Notes

16 Excuses, Excuses, Excuses

Have you ever met someone who has an excuse for everything? An excuse for not becoming, an excuse for not having, an excuse for not doing. Excuses, excuses, excuses! Making an excuse has become so common that it has become a style of communication. However, as a dream-fulfiller, you have to put all excuses aside. Excuses can lead to procrastination, and procrastination can lead to more excuses. Excuses mean dreams that are never dreamt. This section is not designed to scare you, but rather to challenge you to stop making excuses that could send you on a detour from the road to your dream.

According to Webster's dictionary, an excuse is an act of releasing oneself from an obligation or duty. Let's add a twist to this definition. Excuses are self-created exits that release oneself from being obligated to oneself or others.

When my husband and I go to the movies, we go in the main entrance, but when the movie is over, we take the side exit because it is convenient and also to avoid the crowd. Excuses are side exits that people use to avoid the time, energy, commitment, sacrifice and perseverance required to fulfill their dreams.

A dream cannot be left in the hands of an unreliable person. A dream depends on someone who is reliable and sure of himself. It is always questionable whether a dream will become reality if it is left in the hands of an unreliable person. Excuses lessen the chances by weakening your level of accountability and therefore weakening your belief in and pursuit of your dream. The bottom line, dream-fulfillers, is excuses create cowards that are not only afraid to go beyond the norm, but do not feel worthy enough to realize their dreams.

When I was the motivational speaker for a women's organization, the goal during a twelve-week series was to develop a healthy conscience by modifying eating habits and exercising. One of the topics discussed was excuses. During that session, I came up with four reasons why an individual—a dream-fulfiller—needs to overcome excuses:

1. **Excuses put barriers between you and the future**. Excuses can be habit-forming. The first excuse may appear to be appropriate at the time, but I am a firm believer that one excuse leads to another. Eventually, you will find yourself always looking for another excuse to justify the previous excuse you made. Excuses never settle the matter. They only build a barrier that prevents you from seeing what exists on the other side. This is hazardous to you because you eventually can become complacent with what you can see, as opposed to what you cannot see. As a result, the passage that leads to the fulfillment of your dream becomes barred.

2. **Excuses keep us a prisoner of the present**. When you allow excuses to confine you to the present, you relinquish all your rights to obtain what is not. As a result, you become a prisoner of the "what is." What is the "what is"? It is being subject to what you can see, feel, touch, hear and taste right now. The "what is" only sees for what it is now, rather than what it can become. Every time you make an excuse for not fulfilling your dream, more time is added to your present prison sentence. The release date is based solely on your ability to break the habit of excuse-making. Remember, freedom is a choice, so make a decision to stay out of the prison of the present.

3. **Excuses interfere with your being reliable**. It has been proven that people are more apt to listen to a person or buy a product with a good track record. For example, Honda Accord is one of the most reliable vehicles on the market. I can imagine a large number of Hondas are sold on a regular basis. Why? Honda has a track record. Its performance is consistent with the advertisements for the product. I have never heard Honda make an excuse for why it cannot be the number one-selling car. I have never heard Honda's advertisements say, "The reason Honda cannot be the number one-selling car this year is because it has a new competitor." Excuses are not an option for Honda. As a result, Honda maintains its excellent track record and therefore is considered a reliable vehicle.

What does it mean to be reliable? It means to be depended upon with confidence, to be trustworthy and to be consistent. It means to operate within a principle-based environment, where producing results is constant. Honda may modify the style of its car from year to year, but the company's principle-based environment remains the same. This environment did not happen overnight for Honda. In fact, Honda started as a dream. And the success of Honda can be attributed to its founders' ability to rise above excuses (reasons for postponing), and Honda stayed reliable to the fulfillment of their dream.

You must learn to rise above excuses as well, as excuses interfere with your principle-based environment, and that interferes with your reliability. And that interferes with the development of your track record.

Granted, some excuses are valid when it comes to fulfilling your dream. But the fact is once you acknowledged the dream introduced to your thought process, you were held liable to birth your baby—your dream—into reality. If you know anything about being a parent, you have to be reliable. Excuses will not do. An infant does not respond to excuses for not doing. He or she only responds to the action that leads to his or her needs being met.

The same principle applies to the fulfillment of your dream. Your dream does not respond to excuses for not becoming, but only responds to positive action steps that lead to its existence. These steps include meditating, speaking life, setting goals and accomplishing goals. Make this statement, "Away with excuses, and in with actions. I am reliable; therefore, I have a good track record." So dream-fulfillers, stay in your rightful position and be reliable so you can be seen as having a positive track record. Remember, PUSH.

4. **Excuses can cause an infection in your dream**. The fourth reason you should overcome excuses is to prevent an infection from setting into your dream. Remember, an excuse is an act of releasing oneself from an obligation or duty. Excuses distract you from your post and duty, therefore allowing an unwarranted infection (doubt, dream-killers, criticism, etc.) to enter into the confinements of your dream. Once the infection has entered, your dream is exposed to the toxins contained in the infection. If you do not refrain from making excuses, the infection eventually will spread throughout your dream, killing the potential your dream had to become reality. A dream that is dead is soon forgotten.

Recap

1. Excuses are self-created exits that release oneself from being obligated to self or others.

2. Excuses set up barriers between you and the future.

3. Four reasons to overcome excuses:

    (a) They keep you a prisoner of the present.
    (b) They interfere with your being reliable.
    (c) They can cause an infection in your dream that kills the potential of your dream becoming reality.

Thought-provoking Questions

1. What excuse or excuses are preventing you from birthing your dream into reality?

2. From what principle-based environment do you operate?

Notes

Notes

17 Procrastination

There is an old saying, "Never put off until tomorrow what you can do today." What prevents a person from pursuing her dream today, as opposed to tomorrow? Is it the lack of resources? Is it the lack of time? Whatever the reason, procrastination keeps many people from fulfilling their dreams. But once you have set all excuses aside, you can avoid procrastinating on the fulfillment of your dream.

According to Webster's Dictionary, procrastinate is defined as to put off taking action until a future time, to defer or to postpone. This definition implies there is a form of action taking place. When there is motion, there is a process that shifts or moves the person or thing into a different place or position. The process of procrastination works just the opposite. When a person procrastinates fulfilling her dream, her actions produce negative or no results. The process of motion is brought to a halt, and as a result, the individual forfeits herself from excelling to another level. Remember, dreams are inner wants with outer works, so there must be a shift or move taking place inside as well as outside of you to fulfill your dream.

Warning: Procrastination can be habit-forming, and if it's not properly addressed, a person can become complacent in her current position. Remaining in a state of complacency requires the person to constantly make up excuses to substantiate why she has not fulfilled her dream. This is the equation: Procrastination + Excuses = Complacency. Procrastination creates a suitcase of excuses that a person carries around and only unpacks when it comes time to explain the reason for not fulfilling her dream. Excuses such as, "I don't have enough money to go back to school," or "If I am not in New York, I will never make it" cripple a person from going far beyond what she is capable of accomplishing. The accountability she once had toward her dream has depreciated. According to I.V. Hilliard, excuses are self-awarded licenses to remain in your present state of condition.

There are four reasons people procrastinate: 1) The fulfillment of the dream is not a priority; 2) a lack of commitment to self interferes with the commitment to the dream; 3) they are afraid of failure; and 4) they have unclear goals.

The fulfillment of the dream is not a priority. It is not unusual for someone to acknowledge her dream and it not be a priority to fulfill. Many times a dream may be on standby because there are other obligations that take precedence. It is not that a person can't see herself in the future, but she may not be prepared to put forth the effort to reside in the future. For example, Linda is a wife and mother of three. She always has envisioned herself as a high school teacher. However, there are other obligations she must attend to. She has to work part-time to make ends meet. Her children demand a lot of her time. She has duties as a wife. Becoming a teacher is still a dream for Linda, but it is not a priority. Linda may be able to see herself in the future, but her energy and thoughts are channeled more in the present. For all of you who can relate to Linda, you should not force yourself to fulfill your dream, especially if you have other pertinent obligations that need to be addressed.

Anything that is forced becomes a chore, rather than a mission. If this happens, you will not give one hundred percent toward the fulfillment of your dream, and your dream deserves the best. You may ask, "How can taking care of my obligations be considered as procrastination?" In Linda's case, if she becomes complacent in her current condition and begins to use her family obligations to justify not becoming a high school teacher, then she is procrastinating. Linda may be consumed with her family, but she can still do her research by talking to an academic counselor, seeking possible financial assistance and discussing child care or a modification of her husband's schedule to assist her in fulfilling her dream. In other words, at least set a foundation, then build on the dream when the time is right.

A lack of commitment to self interferes with the commitment to the dream. Being in the counseling profession, I have found that people have a hard time being committed to self. People will do for others what they normally would not do for themselves. It is the lack of commitment to self that causes a person to procrastinate fulfilling his dream, and as a result, he settles for just being, rather than becoming. Procrastination becomes a way a person takes pressure off himself when he feels he is in a position to perform.

What prevents someone from being committed to self? It's a lack of the two S's: self-worth and self-esteem. Self-worth is the value placed on one's self, and self-esteem is the impression one has of oneself. Both self-worth and self-esteem are essential from the standpoint that they bring clarity to knowing who you are and the purpose of your existence. When you know who you are, you know where you are going. When you know where you are going, you know what you are capable of doing. The maintenance of your self-worth and self-esteem is an ongoing process that requires you to be committed or, better yet, faithful to yourself. This process of solidifying self not only strengthens the level of commitment to self, but it also creates a source of energy that your dream can plug into to receive life.

People are afraid of failure. The third reason people procrastinate in fulfilling their dreams is they are afraid of failure. Why? First, many people shy away from being in the position to fail because they have the misconception that failure entirely determines their destiny. Failure does not alone determine your destiny. It does, however, reveal your strength. Failure may appear to be defeating, but it does not have to be permanent. Procrastination has become a rescuer for some, and as a result, a lot of untapped dreams remain on the shelves of our minds, collecting dust. Fulfilling a dream is an adventure, and at times there are failures along the way, but the outcome is well worth it.

If you never make a change, you will never know what you are capable of having or doing. When I am pursuing a dream, I picture in my mind that I am on a boat about to leave an island that I am familiar with, my comfort zone. During the course of my travel to the mainland where my dream resides, there are storms, heavy winds and rain, all of which can represent failure. I have a choice, either I can postpone the trip until the conditions are favorable, or I can explore the unknown and endure the storm, winds and rains until I reach the location of my dream.

Second, failure can be scary. It challenges you to come out of your comfort zone. You are so familiar with your comfort zone that you can walk around with your eyes closed because you have acquired senses for that zone. However, when you are pursuing a dream, your old senses won't do. You must acquire new senses that will not be in shock when faced with failure.

The third reason people are afraid of failure is they may not get the proper support. Failure can leave a hurtful residue; therefore, it is essential for the dream-fulfiller to be properly supported by self and/or others when and if failure occurs. Your support system should be able to encourage you to pick yourself up and keep going, critique you by bringing to your attention what you did wrong and what you could have done differently, and direct you by putting you back on the right track to pursuing the dream. A strong support system makes a world of difference when and if you encounter failure.

Goals are not clear. The fourth reason people procrastinate when it comes to fulfilling their dream is their goals are not clearly defined. It's like traveling in fog. There are visibility problems. You have an idea where you're going, but you can't quite see the road. So you have to slow down or even postpone your trip until the fog lifts. Just the same, if your goals are not clear, your dream becomes foggy and your direction unclear. You will move slowly or even postpone moving in a forward direction toward fulfilling your dream.

Recap

1. Why do people procrastinate fulfilling their dreams?
    - The fulfillment of the dream is not a priority.
    - A lack of commitment to self and the dream.
    - They're afraid of failure.
    - They have unclear goals.
2. Procrastination creates a suitcase of excuses that an individual carries around and only unpacks when it comes time to explain the reason for not fulfilling his dream.
3. Excuses + Procrastination = Complacency
4. Failure does not determine your destiny, but it does reveal your strength.
5. Why are people afraid of failure?
    - Misconception of the word "failure" causes people to shy away from being in the position to fail.
    - Failure is scary because it challenges people to come out of their comfort zone.
    - People lack proper support when failure occurs.

Thought-provoking Questions

1. What has caused you to procrastinate in fulfilling your dream?
2. What excuses have you created to convince yourself and others why you have not fulfilled your dream?
3. What has prevented you from being committed to yourself?
4. How do you define failure? How do you respond to it?
5. What type of support group do you have if and when failure does occur?

Dream-fulfiller's Affirmation for Procrastination

I refuse to be a procrastinator. I will not put off tomorrow what I can do today. I will not create a suitcase of excuses that will defer the fulfillment of my dream. I am a dream-fulfiller who is destined for greatness; therefore, I am on a mission, and postponing the fulfillment of my dream is not part of the journey.

Notes

Notes

18 Confidence

S ome wish they had it but do not know the proper channel to receive it. Some people brag about it and even look like they have it, but words can be vain and looks can be deceiving. Some people think they have it but are disappointed when they come up short. Then there are those who do not have to look for it, brag about it or pretend they have it; it's just there. There is a peace on the inside and outside of these people. It is a knowing that an individual possesses that whatever they set their hands to will prosper, whatever they tread they feet on they can have, whatever dream they desire will come to pass. Confidence is what you need. I believe the success of your dream is measured by your level of confidence. Any successful dream-fulfiller knows that the key team player when fulfilling a dream is confidence.

Your dream will always be pending. Why? Confidence is from the inside out, not from the outside in. This is why you cannot measure an individual's level of confidence by his outer appearance. Confidence is an inward knowing. This section will answer these questions: 1) What is confidence; 2) How do I obtain confidence; 3) What are the signs of confidence?; and 4) What can come against confidence?

What is Confidence?

Confidence is defined as having full trust or belief in the reliability of a person or thing. It is an inward knowing that supercedes an outward condition. For example, the confidence a person has placed in his car is not only based on the ability of the car to transport him to his desired destination, but also to provide the performance needed during uncomfortable and/or hazardous weather conditions.

After conducting business in the hot scorching sun, someone would have confidence in the air conditioner producing an atmosphere that is more favorable in the car. There is an inward knowing that the performance of the car supercedes the outward condition. During the rainy season, the roads are normally slippery and the visibility is low. Someone would expect her car to be durable enough (i.e. air-tight, windshield wipers in check, etc.) to withstand the rain. There is an inward knowing that the performance of the car supercedes the outward condition. Each time the car validates its reliability, a person's confidence level increases.

Dream-fulfillers, every time you make a deposit, every time you invest in your inner man, you are building up your confidence level. When you are confident in your inner man, what you are saying is:

1. I am confident that my inner man will protect and nurture my unique abilities.

2. I am confident that my inner man will release my unique abilities through my physical actions at the appropriate time.

3. I am confident that I can withdraw strength from my inner man to overcome opposition.

How Do You Obtain Confidence?

By constantly pouring life (i.e. reading books, listening to tapes and associating with positive people) into your inner man so you can withdraw the strength needed to push your dream into reality. By constantly speaking life so you are confirming what you have deposited into your inner man, in addition to lining up your physical actions with the inner man. By constantly believing in what you have deposited into your inner man until you see the manifestation of your dream. If you pour, you shall fill. If you speak, you shall create. And if you believe, you shall receive. Once you obtain your confidence, hold on to it because you will be richly rewarded.

What Are The signs Of Confidence?

When you declare that you are confident, signs should follow. It is one thing to say, "I am confident," but it is another thing to have evidence that confirms your confidence. Just as a lawyer needs evidence to prove the innocence of his clients, you need evidence to prove your ability to be confident while fulfilling your dream. There are five signs indicating when you are confident:

1. **When you do not succumb to pressure**. Have you ever been between a rock and a hard place? That's pressure! I have found that everyone handles pressure differently. Some people back off when they are under pressure. Some people give up when they are under pressure. Some people get nervous when they are under pressure. But some people do not succumb to pressure. They are confident in who they are, what they are doing and where they are going. Not only are they confident about their existence and purpose, but they also realize that fulfilling a dream is a process. It would be foolish to say that confident people do not encounter pressure, but their positive attitude clearly states that they refuse to succumb to pressure. I believe pressure has the right to exist, but I also believe I have the right to refuse to be under pressure. So what does it mean to succumb? And what is pressure? To succumb is to relinquish control or to surrender to thoughts, criticisms, suggestions, circumstances, causing premature decisions to be made. To apply pressure is to force someone or something to release or produce results or evidence at a needed time. So to succumb to pressure is to relinquish your rights or to surrender to external stimuli that force you to release or produce results or evidence that is not in sync with the process that already has been established for the fulfillment of your dream. In other words, you are put into a position to rush.

A confident dream-fulfiller understands and respects the dream-fulfillment process and is less likely to become desperate while pursuing her dream. Pressure or process—the choice is yours.

2. **When you know you have rights**. Have you ever met someone who did not know his rights? His conversations, actions, thoughts and, yes, his lifestyle conveys that he is in bondage to tradition (physically, mentally, emotionally, and financially). It is sad to say that a lot of people have settled and keep settling because they did not and they do not know their rights. What rights? The right to be healthy, the right to be prosperous, the right to internal and external peace, the right to be whole and complete in this lifetime, the right to have dreams manifested.

Only those who are confident will reap the full benefits of dream-fulfillment. They have acquired an attitude that demands their rights. It is effortless for a confident dream-fulfiller to speak life because he knows his right. It is easy for a confident dream-fulfiller to make sacrifices because he knows his rights. It is easy for a confident dream-fulfiller to go against the odds because he knows his rights. Whatever a confident dream-fulfiller decides upon, then declares will be established unto him because he knows his rights. So PUSH!

3. **Believe even when you don't see results**. Not everybody can do this. For many people, this can be challenging. How do I know? Been there. We live in such a realistic society that bases believing on seeing. As a result, people have unconsciously adopted this ideology as fact; therefore, they deny themselves the opportunity to experience the extraordinary. Well, I would like to debate this ideology by stating that believing is a form of seeing that has not been revealed to your physical senses. Only confident dream-fulfillers can comprehend this type of believing. They understand believing is an intricate part of the dream-fulfillment process. During the process, a dream-fulfiller always will deposit enriching information in his inner man, and in return, it reinforces what he believes. So when a dream-fulfiller does not see anything in the physical realm, that's okay because a visual picture already has been drawn within his inner man. This visual picture is sufficient enough to sustain the dream-fulfiller until the dream becomes a physical reality. A confident dream-fulfiller knows if he does not see results today, he will eventually see results if he keeps pushing. So PUSH!

4. **You are willing to make sacrifices**. What sacrifices are you willing to make? Any dream you desire to obtain will require you to make them. No one said sacrificing is easy or comfortable. It is an adjustment. I like to view sacrificing as voluntarily surrendering or relinquishing something or someone of value to advance in life. To make it short and simple, sacrifices are choice-driven. You can choose to sacrifice and avail yourself to more possibilities to further your dream. If you choose to sacrifice, you have automatically set into motion opportunities to see your birthing process reach its term on time and healthy.

On the other hand, you can choose not to sacrifice, and get the opposite effect. Sacrificing will challenge you not only to hunger and embrace something new, but also to do things you do not necessarily want to do to achieve things you desire. I will sacrifice today, but I will gain tomorrow. I will sacrifice what I am used to, but I will gain something I never had. The reason sacrificing is a sign of confidence is the discipline, commitment and passion the dream-fulfiller has obtained that puts her in the position to receive the maximum results of her dream-fulfillment. Confident dream-fulfillers are willing to do things today that others are not willing to do, and confident dream-fulfillers will have things tomorrow that others will not have. Therefore, it is better to sacrifice.

5. **You are willing to share with others**. As a dream-fulfiller, you automatically put yourself in the position of being a mentor. Most likely, you did not apply for this position, nor did you volunteer, but it comes with the territory. You do not have to be flamboyant for people to recognize your confidence. Confidence has its own magnetic force that draws people who not only admire but want to emulate the positive demeanor you display. A confident dream-fulfiller does not feel threatened or vulnerable when disclosing to others his personal victories and defeats in the dream-fulfillment process. I am confident in what I share with others because I am confident in what I deposit into my inner man. So PUSH!

What Can Come Up Against Your Confidence?

Confidence is a priceless jewel and should be protected at all times. Confidence should never be taken for granted. It is confidence that sustains you while you are waiting for the manifestation of your dream.

It is the responsibility of the dream-fulfiller to recognize and avoid all intruders that attempt to come up against your confidence. Intruders are specially designed to destroy your confidence by entering into your inner man and replacing positive information with negative information. Once the inner man has been contaminated, the inner strength that fuels your confidence is shut off. When there is no confidence, the possibilities become impossible, and the dream is just a mere thought. There are three intruders that a dream-fulfiller should be aware of.

Intruder #1: Words. I cannot place enough emphasis on the power of words. What you say will determine what you will be, what you will have and where you will go. If your words carry that much weight, what type of repercussion do the words of others (i.e. friends, family, peers, etc.) have on your life? A lot. Dream-fulfiller, you need to guard your inner man with all diligence. Everyone cannot speak into your life. The words that are released from the mouths of others can be detrimental to your dream. By sitting amid unhealthy conversations filled with doubt and disbelief, you are not only consenting, but you are submitting to the thoughts and beliefs of others. The process of assimilation begins to occur, causing your confidence level to reduce to that of your peers. Remember, victory and defeat are in the power of the tongue, so choose your words and your friends wisely.

Intruder #2: Failure. Who hasn't experienced failure at one time or another in her life? Failure can be embarrassing, disappointing and painful, but I assure you it is definitely not the end of the world. Failure was not designed for you to close the theater curtain and cancel the show, but to re-evaluate and rewrite the script as needed and get back to work.

Think about it, there are millionaires who go bankrupt every day. They do not throw in the towel just because their businesses failed, but rather they start up another million-dollar business and change the name from JB Corporation to BJ Corporation. In other words, failure did not destroy their confidence. Why? Their inner knowing supercedes the outer conditions. Failing is not the problem for most people; it is their inability to maintain the high confidence level they had before the failure occurred. If not treated properly, the residue from the failure can penetrate through the inner man, leaving behind a stain. As a result, confidence becomes shattered, dreams become distant, and life's direction becomes undefined. Remember, failure is not designed for a setback, but only for a comeback. So PUSH!

Intruder #3: Insecurity. Why is it that we as humans have the biggest problem accepting who we are? We are either too fat or too thin, too short or too tall, and the list can go on and on. Look at a dog. What can be more proud than a dog? A dog can be mixed two-hundred times. You will never see a dog hold his head down simply because he is a mutt, but instead the dog struts down the street with confidence. I am not comparing you with a dog, but I do wonder why humans are so insecure. Perhaps it's the lack of being self-differentiated. When a person is self-differentiated, he is able to establish his own identity, opinions and/or thoughts independent of those around him, creating an autonomous identity. However, a person who is not self-differentiated depends on the identity, opinions and thoughts of others to determine his existence. He lacks the ability to detach from the identity of others, creating insecurity. A person who is constantly controlled by his insecurity can never be confident due to the fact that his life always depends on the opinions, decisions and thoughts of others.

Recap

1. What is confidence? It is an inward knowing that supercedes any outward condition.

2. Confidence is from the inside out, not from the outside in.

3. How do you obtain confidence?
    a) By constantly pouring life into your inner man.
    b) By constantly speaking life so you are confirming what you have deposited into your inner man.
    c) By constantly believing in what you have deposited into your inner man.

4. Five signs you are confident:

a) When you do not succumb to pressure

b) When you know you have rights.

c) When you believe even when you do not see results.

d) When you are willing to make sacrifices.

e) When you are willing to share with others.

5. What can come up against confidence? There are three intruders that a dream-fulfiller should be aware of:

a) Words.

b) Failure.

c) Insecurity.

Thought-provoking Questions

1. Name two things about yourself that show confidence?

2. What has come up against your confidence in the past? And how did you handle it?

A Dreamer's Affirmation on Confidence

I refuse to be agitated and disturbed. I will not allow myself to be intimidated, fearful, cowardly, or unsettled. I am grounded, settled and fixed in what I believe to be true; therefore, I will stake my claim daily to what rightfully belongs to me. I will be anxious for nothing, for my dream will come to pass at the appointed time. I am confident in this.

Notes

Notes

19 Words of Wisdom

I wish someone had shared with me what I am about to share with you in this chapter. I had to learn from experience. I would like to leave you, a dream-fulfiller, with some advice: Never depend on your senses or your feelings to determine the outcome of your dream. Both your senses and your feelings either serve to alert you or suggest to you how to respond to a particular event and/or situation. Although we need our senses to function daily and we depend on our feelings to make judgments and decisions, when it comes to fulfilling our dream, our senses or feelings are not the determining factor.

In fact, our senses and feelings are limited to the point that they can only keep us abreast of the here and now—never the future. As a dream-fulfiller, you must realize that when your dream transforms into a desire, it should no longer be influenced by your senses or feelings. Now it resides in your inner man, which operates from a different realm. It is the inner man that understands the importance of your dream and therefore surrounds your desire with diligence, determination, passion, perseverance, long suffering and patience.

Your physical being has been conditioned to operate within the realm of your senses and feelings. So when your mind is exposed to a visual picture of you in the future, and it drops down into the inner man, your senses and/or feelings send up red flags indicating that something is going against the gradient, and automatically, you are faced with resistance.

Both your senses and feelings join forces in an effort to convince, coach, even rearrange your thoughts into believing that your dream is unrealistic and impossible to obtain. And if you ponder long enough, you become passive, weak and doubtful, and your dream will never have a chance to become reality. You must train your mind to bypass your senses and feelings and stay connected with the inner man that is pregnant with the desire. So when you cannot touch the marble floor of your new dream house, go beyond the sense of touch. When you cannot see people standing in line to get into your restaurant, go beyond the sense of sight.

When you have not tasted the results of your best-selling recipe, go beyond the sense of taste. When you cannot hear your song playing on the radio, go beyond the sense of sound. And when you do not feel like going the extra mile to reach your dream, go beyond your feelings. Remember, PUSH! And don't stop pushing until your dream is born.

A Dreamer's Affirmation for Wisdom

I choose to operate in wisdom. I will seek wise counseling from those who have fulfilled their dreams. As I walk in the presence of the wise, I will glean from them. I have creative, insightful wisdom that challenges me to seek and possess the skills I need to live a successful life. With wisdom, I will tap into the goals and plans I will use to make my dream become reality. Wisdom is my guide into the future; therefore, I will inhale wisdom and exhale results.

Notes

Notes

20 Dream-Fulfiller's Regiment

Once you are operating in wisdom, you need to stay in the habit of doing so. I have heard that it takes twenty-one days to form a habit. That is not a lot of time, but during those twenty-one days, you need a lot of discipline. Discipline is the key to being a successful dream-fulfiller. I have created the following pages that will assist you in developing the structure you need to gain the maximum results of the dream-fulfillment process. This dream-fulfiller's regiment will help you remain disciplined. It will provide you with a time frame for daily affirmations and meditation time. You also will be able to write down your goals for the day as it relates to your dream, and determine the progress you have made at the end of the day.

I recommend you work at least thirty minutes to two hours per day toward the fulfillment of your dream (i.e. reading a book about your dream, writing up a business plan, writing two to three pages a day on your book, going out every day and looking for your dream home, etc.). If you can work your job eight to ten hours a day, you should be able to spare at least thirty minutes for yourself and your dream (unless your dream is your job).

Used daily, this dream-fulfiller's regiment will help you assess the progress you are making toward obtaining your dream. It is vital that you use these pages to record valuable information that will help you discover a regiment that works best for you. There is only one dream-fulfillment process, but there are different regiments that can be used during the process. Don't forget to PUSH that baby—your dream—into reality.

DREAM-FULFILLER'S REGIMENT

Day 1

Morning (6 to 6:05 a.m.):

Dream-fulfiller's Affirmation: *I choose to have an attitude of expectancy. I have the patience and the composure needed to look beyond what I can see, while waiting for what I cannot see. I choose to be committed. I choose to be settled because I am convinced that the manifestation I am waiting for belongs to me. My attitude determines my altitude; therefore, I choose to have an attitude of expectancy.*

Meditate on your dream. (Note: It would help if you had a dreamscape board with pictures. If not, your imagination will work fine.)

Today's Goals:

1. _____

2. _____

3. _____

Midday (Noon to 12:05 p.m.):

Dream-fulfiller's Affirmation: *I choose to put pressure on my mouth. I choose to discipline my mouth to speak words that bring life to my dream. I choose to put pressure on my mouth to speak words that are in line and in agreement with the language of the invisible realm. I choose to put pressure on my mouth so I will continually pull what I cannot see into existence. I choose to put pressure on my mouth so my mind stays in tune with my inner man, and my feelings and emotions remain under subjection at all times. I believe; therefore, I put pressure on my mouth and speak.*

Meditate on your dream.

Evening (6 to 6:05 p.m.):

Dream-fulfiller's Affirmation: *I refuse to be agitated and disturbed. I will not allow myself to be intimidated, fearful, cowardly or unsettled. I am grounded, settled and fixed in what I believe to be true; therefore, I stake my claim daily to what rightfully belongs to me. I will be anxious for nothing, for my dream will come to pass at the appointed time.*

Meditate on your dream.

Review Progress:

1. What goals were completed today?
2. What goals were not completed? Why not?
3. What distractions did you face today while pursuing your dream? How did you handle those distractions?
4. What type of bacteria tried to invade your environment? What solvent did you use to kill the bacteria?
5. Are you satisfied with the progress you made toward the fulfillment of your dream today? If so, why? If not, why?

Total hours spent towards fulfilling your dream_____

Dream-fulfiller's Regiment

Day 2

Morning (6 to 6:05 a.m.):

Dream-fulfiller's Affirmation: *I choose to put pressure on my mouth. I choose to discipline my mouth to speak words that bring life to my dream. I choose to put pressure on my mouth to speak words that are in line and in agreement with the language of the invisible realm. I choose to put pressure on my mouth so I will continually pull into existence what I cannot see. I choose to put pressure on my mouth so my mind stays in tune with my inner man, and my feelings and emotions remain under subjection at all times. I believe; therefore, I will put pressure on my mouth and speak.*

Meditate on your dream. (Meditation + Affirmation = Manifestation)

Today's Goals:

1. _____

2. _____

3. _____

Midday (Noon to 12:05 p.m.):

Dream-fulfiller's Affirmation: *I choose to put pressure on my mouth. I choose to discipline my mouth to speak words that bring life to my dream. I choose to put pressure on my mouth to speak words that are in line and in agreement with the language of the invisible realm. I choose to put pressure on my mouth so I will continually pull into existence what I cannot see. I choose to put pressure on my mouth so my mind stays in tune with my inner man, and my feelings and emotions remain under subjection at all times. I believe; therefore, I will put pressure on my mouth to speak.*

Meditate on your dream.

Evening (6 to 6:05 p.m.):

Dream-fulfiller's Affirmation: *I choose to put pressure on my mouth. I choose to discipline my mouth to speak words that bring life to my dream. I choose to put pressure on my mouth to speak words that are in line and in agreement with the language of the invisible realm. I choose to put pressure on my mouth so I will continually pull into existence what I cannot see. I choose to put pressure on my mouth so my mind stays in tune with my inner man, and my feelings and emotions remain under subjection at all times. I believe; therefore, I will put pressure on my mouth to speak.*

Meditate on your dream.

Review Progress:

1. What goals were completed today?

2. What goals were not completed? Why not?

3. What distractions did you face today while pursuing your dream? How did you handle those distractions?

4. What type of bacteria tried to invade your environment? What solvent did you use to kill the bacteria?

5. Are you satisfied with the progress you made toward your dream today? If so, why? If not, why?

Total hours spent towards fulfilling your dream_____

DREAM-FULFILLER'S REGIMENT

DAY 3

Morning (6 to 6:05 a.m.):

Dream-fulfiller's Affirmation: *I refuse to be agitated and disturbed. I will not allow myself to be intimidated, fearful, cowardly or unsettled. I am grounded, settled and fixed in what I believe to be true; therefore, I will stake my claim daily to what rightfully belongs to me. I will be anxious for nothing, for my dream will come to pass at the appointed time.*

Meditate on your dream. (Meditation acknowledges the invisible realm.)

Today's Goals:

1. _____

2. _____

3. _____

Midday (Noon to 12:05 p.m.):

Dream-fulfiller's Affirmation: *I refuse to be agitated and disturbed. I will not allow myself to be intimidated, fearful, cowardly or unsettled. I am grounded, settled and fixed in what I believe to be true; therefore, I will stake my claim daily to what rightfully belongs to me. I will be anxious for nothing, for my dream will come to pass at the appointed time.*

Mediate on your dream.

Evening (6 to 6:05 p.m.):

Dream-fulfiller's Affirmation: *I refuse to be agitated and disturbed. I will not allow myself to be intimidated, fearful, cowardly or unsettled. I am grounded, settled and fixed in what I believe to be true; therefore, I will stake my claim daily to what rightfully belongs to me. I will be anxious for nothing, for my dream will come to pass at the appointed time.*

Meditate on your dream.

Review Progress:

1. What goals were completed?

2. What goals were not completed? Why not?

3. What distractions did you face today while pursuing your dream? How did you handle the distractions?

4. What type of bacteria tried to invade your environment? What solvent did you use to kill the bacteria?

5. Are you satisfied with the progress you made toward your dream today? If so, why? If not, why?

Total hours spent towards fulfilling your dream_____

DREAM-FULFILLER'S REGIMENT

Day 4

Morning (6 to 6:05 a.m.):

Dream-fulfiller's Affirmation: *I have the mind of a dream-fulfiller who instructs his or her mouth and adds learning and persuasiveness to his or her lips.*

Meditate on your dream.
(Meditation is seeing things that are not as though they were.)

Today's Goals:

1. _____

2. _____

3. _____

Midday (Noon to 12:05 p.m.):

Dream-fulfiller's Affirmation: *I have the mind of a dream-fulfiller who instructs his or her mouth and adds learning and persuasiveness to his or her lips.*

Meditate on your dream.

Evening (6 to 6:05 p.m.):

Dream-fulfiller's Affirmation: *I have the mind of a dream-fulfiller who instructs his or her mouth and adds learning and persuasiveness to his or her lips.*

Meditate on your dream.

Review Progress:

1. What goals were completed?

2. What goals were not completed? Why not?

3. What distractions did you face today while pursuing your dream? How did you handle the distractions?

4. What type of bacteria tried to invade your environment? What solvent did you use to kill the bacteria?

5. Are you satisfied with the progress you made toward the fulfillment of your dream today? If so, why? If not, why?

Total hours spent towards fulfilling your dream_____

DREAM-FULFILLER'S REGIMENT

Day 5

Morning (6 to 6:05 a.m.):

Dream-fulfiller's Affirmation: *I will speak only the words that have the ability to paint the inner image I need on the inside of me to obtain the dream I desire to see manifested into reality. My inner image is in harmony with my dream, and my physical actions are in harmony with my inner image; therefore, I have dominion.*

Meditate on your dream.
(Meditation is a job, so get to work!)

Midday (Noon to 12:05 p.m.):

Dream-fulfiller's Affirmation: *I will speak only the words that have the ability to paint the inner image I need on the inside of me to obtain the dream I desire to see manifested into reality. My inner image is in harmony with my dream, and my physical actions are in harmony with my inner image; therefore, I have dominion.*

Mediate on your dream.

Evening (6 to 6:05 p.m.):

Dream-fulfiller's Affirmation: *I will speak only the words that have the ability to paint the inner image I need on the inside of me to obtain the dream I desire to see manifested into reality. My inner image is in harmony with my dream, and my physical actions are in harmony with my inner image; therefore, I have dominion.*

Meditate on your dream.

Review Progress:
1. What goals were completed?
2. What goals were not completed? Why not?
3. What distractions did you face today while pursuing your dream? How did you handle the distractions?

4. What type of bacteria tried to invade your environment? What solvent did you use to kill the bacteria?

5. Are you satisfied with the progress you made toward the fulfillment of your dream today? If so, why? If not, why?

Total hours spent towards fulfilling your dream_____

DREAM-FULFILLER'S REGIMENT

Day 6

Morning (6 to 6:05 a.m.):

Dream-fulfiller's Affirmation: *I will not indulge in watching unproductive television shows. I highly respect my inner man and the information that is contained within. I will be wise and prudent in selecting the television shows that reinforce the inner image that exists within me.*

Today's Goals:

1. _____

2. _____

3. _____

Meditate on your dream.
(A mind that is disciplined removes doubt and fear.)

Midday (Noon to 12:05 p.m.):

Dream-fulfiller's Affirmation: *I will not indulge in unproductive television shows. I highly respect my inner man and the information that is contained within. I will be wise and prudent in selecting the television shows that reinforce the inner image that exists within me.*

Meditate on your dream.

Evening (6 to 6:05 p.m.):

Dream-fulfiller's Affirmation: *I will not indulge in unproductive television shows. I highly respect my inner man and the information that is contained within. I will be wise and prudent in selecting the television shows that reinforce the inner image that exists within me.*

Meditate on your dream.

Review Progress:

1. What goals were completed?

2. What goals were not completed? Why not?

3. What distractions did you face today while pursuing your dream? How did you handle the distractions?

4. What type of bacteria tried to invade your environment? What solvent did you use to kill the bacteria?

5. Are you satisfied with the progress you made toward the fulfillment of your dream today? If so, why? If not, why?

Total hours spent towards fulfilling your dream____

DREAM-FULFILLER'S REGIMENT

Day 7

Morning (6 to 6:05 a.m.):

Dream-fulfiller's Affirmation: *I believe and accept that my dream (say what your dream is) is manifesting into reality. I am not moved by what I see or feel. I am only moved by the words that speak life into my dream. I believe; therefore, I will continue to speak my dream into existence.*

Meditate on your dream.
(A mind that wanders is a mind that is left unsupervised.)

Today's Goals:

1. _____

2. _____

3. _____

Midday (Noon to 12:05 p.m.):

Dream-fulfiller's Affirmation: *I believe and accept that my dream (say what your dream is) is manifesting into reality. I am not moved by what I see or feel. I am only moved by the words that speak life into my dream. I believe; therefore, I will continue to speak my dream into existence.*

Meditate on your dream.

Evening (6 to 6:05 p.m.):

Dream-fulfiller's Affirmation: *I believe and accept that my dream (say what your dream is) is manifesting into reality. I am not moved by what I see or feel. I am only moved by the words that speak life into my dream. I believe; therefore, I will continue to speak my dream into existence.*

Meditate on your dream.

Review Progress:

1. What goals were completed?

2. What goals were not completed? Why not?

3. What distractions did you face today while pursuing your dream? How did you handle the distractions?

4. What type of bacteria tried to invade your environment? What solvent did you use to kill the bacteria?

5. Are you satisfied with the progress you made toward the fulfillment of your dream today? If so, why? If not, why?

Total hours spent towards fulfilling your dream_____

DREAM-FULFILLER'S REGIMENT

Day 8

Morning (6 to 6:05 a.m.):

Dream-fulfiller's Affirmation: *I choose to deposit words of life into my inner man, for it is my inner man that contains the words that determine my destiny. My inner man is implanted and rooted with words that have the power to keep my mind in line and in agreement with my dream.*

Meditate on your dream.
(Meditation is a gift, so open up the package and put it to use.)

Today's Goals:

1. _____

2. _____

3. _____

Midday (Noon to 12:05 p.m.):

Dream-fulfiller's Affirmation: *I choose to deposit words of life into my inner man, for it is my inner man that contains the words that determine my destiny. My inner man is implanted and rooted with words that have the power to keep my mind in line and in agreement with my dream.*

Meditate on your dream.

Evening (6 to 6:05 p.m.):

Dream-fulfiller's Affirmation: *I choose to deposit words of life into my inner man, for it is my inner man that contains the words that determine my destiny. My inner man is implanted and rooted with words that have the power to keep my mind in line and in agreement with my dream.*

Meditate on your dream.

Review Progress:

1. What goals were completed?

2. What goals were not completed? Why not?

3. What distractions did you face today while pursuing your dream? How did you handle the distractions?

4. What type of bacteria tried to invade your environment? What solvent did you use to kill the bacteria?

5. Are you satisfied with the progress you made toward the fulfillment of your dream today? If so, why? If not, why?

Total hours spent towards fulfilling your dream_____

DREAM-FULFILLER'S REGIMENT

Day 9

Morning (6 to 6:05 a.m.):

Dream-fulfiller's Affirmation: *Victory and defeat are in the power of the tongue, and those who indulge in them will eat the fruit of them, whether victory or defeat.*

Mediate on your dream.
(Meditation strengthens your faith.)

Today's Goals:

1. _____

2. _____

3. _____

Midday (Noon to 12:05 p.m.):

Dream-fulfiller's Affirmation: *Victory and defeat are in the power of the tongue, and those who indulge in them will eat the fruit of them, whether victory or defeat.*

Meditate on your dream.

Evening (6 to 6:05 p.m.):

Dream-fulfiller's Affirmation: *Victory and defeat are in the power of the tongue, and those who indulge in them will eat the fruit of them, whether victory or defeat.*

Meditate on your dream.

Review Progress:
1. What goals were completed?
2. What goals were not completed? Why not?

3. What distractions did you face today while pursuing your dream? How did you handle the distractions?

4. What type of bacteria tried to invade your environment? What solvent did you use to kill the bacteria?

5. Are you satisfied with the progress you made toward the fulfillment of your dream today? If so, why? If not, why?

Total hours spent towards fulfilling your dream_____

DREAM-FULFILLER'S REGIMENT

Day 10

Morning (6 to 6:05 a.m.):

Dream-fulfiller's Affirmation: *I am the victor and not the victim of the trial; therefore, I refuse to be subject to what the trial presents to me. I will only speak the solution, not the problem. I am a dream-fulfiller who will ride the storm. I will soar in high places where my dream resides.*

Meditate on your dream.
(Meditation disciplines your mind to stay in line with your inner man.)

Today's Goals:

1. _____

2. _____

3. _____

Midday (Noon to 12:05 p.m.):

Dream-fulfiller's Affirmation: *I am the victor and not the victim of the trial; therefore, I refuse to be subject to what the trial presents to me. I will only speak the solution, not the problem. I am a dream-fulfiller who will ride the storm. I will soar in high places where my dream resides.*

Meditate on your dream.

Evening (6 to 6:05 p.m.):

Dream-fulfiller's Affirmation: *I am the victor and not the victim of the trial; therefore, I refuse to be subject to what the trial presents to me. I will only speak the solution, not the problem. I am a dream-fulfiller who will ride the storm. I will soar in high places where my dream resides.*

Meditate on your dream.

Review Progress:
1. What goals were completed?

2. What goals were not completed? Why not?

3. What distractions did you face today while pursuing your dream? How did you handle the distractions?

4. What type of bacteria tried to invade your environment? What solvent did you use to kill the bacteria?

5. Are you satisfied with the progress you made toward the fulfillment of your dream today? If so, why? If not, why?

Total hours spent towards fulfilling your dream_____

DREAM–FULFILLER'S REGIMENT

Day 11

Morning (6 to 6:05 a.m.):

Dream-fulfiller's Affirmation: *I choose to reprogram my mind on a daily basis. I will only expose my thought process to people, places and things that are beneficial to the fulfillment of my dream. I will think about whatever is positive. I will think about whatever is productive. I will dictate my thoughts and not let my thoughts dictate me. My dream will not drown in negative, defeated thoughts, but it will swim in thoughts that line up with my dream. I always will know what is upstairs because I refuse to let my mind be downstairs.*

Meditate on your dream.
(Meditation is a mode of transportation to your destiny.)

Today's Goals:

1. _____

2. _____

3. _____

Midday (Noon to 12:05 p.m.):

Dream-fulfiller's Affirmation: I choose to reprogram my mind on a daily basis. I will only expose my thought process to people, places and things that are beneficial to the fulfillment of my dream. I will think about whatever is positive. I will think about whatever is productive. I will dictate my thoughts and not let my thoughts dictate me. My dream will not drown in negative, defeated thoughts, but it will swim in thoughts that line up with my dream. I always will know what is upstairs because I refuse to let my mind be downstairs.

Meditate on your dream.

Evening (6 to 6:05 p.m.):

Dream-fulfiller's Affirmation: *I choose to reprogram my mind on a daily basis. I will only expose my thought process to people, places and things that are beneficial to the fulfillment of my dream. I will think about whatever is positive. I will think about whatever is productive. I will dictate my thoughts and not let my thoughts dictate me. My dream will not drown in negative, defeated thoughts, but it will swim in thoughts that line up with my dream. I always will know what is upstairs because I refuse to let my mind be downstairs.*

Meditate on your dream.

Review Progress:

1. What goals were completed?

2. What goals were not completed? Why not?

3. What distractions did you face today while pursuing your dream? How did you handle the distractions?

4. What type of bacteria tried to invade your environment? What solvent did you use to kill the bacteria?

5. Are you satisfied with the progress you made toward the fulfillment of your dream today? If so, why? If not, why?

Total hours spent towards fulfilling your dream_____

DREAM-FULFILLER'S REGIMENT

Day 12

Morning (6 to 6:05 a.m.):

Dream-fulfiller's Affirmation: *I choose to believe in myself. I am unique, whole and special. I am aware of what I am capable of doing or having because I know and believe in myself. I choose to have confidence in myself because I know that the success of my dream depends on me.*

Meditate on your dream.
(A dweller always dwells in the future.)

Today's Goals:

1. _____

2. _____

3. _____

Midday (Noon to 12:05 p.m.):

Dream-fulfiller's Affirmation: *I choose to believe in myself. I am unique, whole and special. I am aware of what I am capable of doing or having because I know and believe in myself. I choose to have confidence in myself because I know that the success of my dream depends on me.*

Meditate on your dream.

Evening (6 to 6:05 p.m.):

Dream-fulfiller's Affirmation: *I choose to believe in myself. I am unique, whole and special. I am aware of what I am capable of doing or having because I know and believe in myself. I choose to have confidence in myself because I know that the success of my dream depends on me.*

Meditate on your dream.

Review Progress:

1. What goals were completed?

2. What goals were not completed? Why not?

3. What distractions did you face today while pursuing your dream? How did you handle the distractions?

4. What type of bacteria tried to invade your environment? What solvent did you use to kill the bacteria?

5. Are you satisfied with the progress you made toward the fulfillment of your dream today? If so, why? If not, why?

Total hours spent towards fulfilling your dream_____

DREAM-FULFILLER'S REGIMENT

Day 13

Morning (6 to 6:05 a.m.):

Dream-fulfiller's Affirmation: *I am pregnant with being/having*_____ *(state your dream), and I promise myself and my dream that I will protect, nurture and love my dream at all times. I will speak life into my dream every day. I will make the preparations needed to cultivate my dream into becoming reality.*

Meditate on your dream.
(A dream that is remembered will never die.)

Today's Goals:

1. _____

2. _____

3. _____

Midday (Noon to 12:05 p.m.):

Dream-fulfiller's Affirmation: *I am pregnant with being/having*_____ *(state your dream), and I promise myself and my dream that I will protect, nurture and love my dream at all times. I will speak life into my dream every day. I will make the preparations needed to cultivate my dream into becoming reality.*

Meditate on your dream.

Evening (6 to 6:05 p.m.):

Dream-fulfiller's Affirmation: *I am pregnant with being/having*_____ *(state your dream), and I promise myself and my dream that I will protect, nurture and love my dream at all times. I will speak life into my dream every day. I will make the preparations needed to cultivate my dream into becoming reality.*

Meditate on your dream.

Review Progress:
1. What goals were completed?
2. What goals were not completed? Why not?
3. What distractions did you face today while pursuing your dream? How did you handle the distractions?
4. What type of bacteria tried to invade your environment? What solvent did you use to kill the bacteria?
5. Are you satisfied with the progress you made toward the fulfillment of your dream today? If so, why? If not, why?

Total hours spent towards fulfilling your dream_____

DREAM-FULFILLER'S REGIMENT

Day 14

Morning (6 to 6:10 a.m.):

Dream-fulfiller's Affirmation: *I refuse to be a procrastinator. I will not put off until tomorrow what I can do today. I will not create a suitcase of excuses that will defer the fulfillment of my dream. I am a dream-fulfiller who is destined for greatness; therefore, I am on a mission, and postponing fulfillment of my dream is not part of the journey.*

Meditate on your dream.
(If you can see it, you can have it.)

Today's Goals:

1. _____

2. _____

3. _____

Midday (Noon to 12:10 p.m.):

Dream-fulfiller's Affirmation: *I refuse to be a procrastinator. I will not put off until tomorrow what I can do today. I will not create a suitcase of excuses that will defer the fulfillment of my dream. I am a dream-fulfiller who is destined for greatness; therefore, I am on a mission, and postponing fulfillment of my dream is not part of the journey.*

Meditate on your dream.

Evening (6 to 6:05 p.m.):

Dream-fulfiller's Affirmation: *I refuse to be a procrastinator. I will not put off until tomorrow what I can do today. I will not create a suitcase of excuses that will defer the fulfillment of my dream. I am a dream-fulfiller who is destined for greatness; therefore, I am on a mission, and postponing fulfillment of my dream is not part of the journey.*

Meditate on your dream.

Review Progress:

1. What goals were completed?

2. What goals were not completed? Why not?

3. What distractions did you face today while pursuing your dream? How did you handle the distractions?

4. What type of bacteria tried to invade your environment? What solvent did you use to kill the bacteria?

5. Are you satisfied with the progress you made toward the fulfillment of your dream today? If so, why? If not, why?

Total hours spent towards fulfilling your dream_____

DREAM-FULFILLER'S REGIMENT

Day 15

Morning (6 to 6:10 a.m.):

Dream-fulfiller's Affirmation: *I choose to operate in wisdom. I will seek wise counseling from those who have fulfilled their dreams. As I walk in the presence of the wise, I will gleam from them. I have creative, insightful wisdom that challenges me to seek and possess the skills I need to live a successful life. With wisdom, I will tap into the goals and plans I will use to make my dream become reality. Wisdom is my guide into the future; therefore, I will inhale wisdom and exhale results.*

Meditate on your dream.
(Dream as if your life depends on it, because it does.)

Today's Goals:

1. _____

2. _____

3. _____

Midday (Noon to 12:10 p.m.):

Dream-fulfiller's Affirmation: I choose to operate in wisdom. I will seek wise counseling from those who have fulfilled their dreams. As I walk in the presence of the wise, I will gleam from them. I have creative, insightful wisdom that challenges me to seek and possess the skills I need to live a successful life. With wisdom, I will tap into the goals and plans I will use to make my dream become reality. Wisdom is my guide into the future; therefore, I will inhale wisdom and exhale results.

Meditate on your dream.

Evening (6 to 6:05 p.m.):

Dream-fulfiller's Affirmation: *I choose to operate in wisdom. I will seek wise counseling from those who have fulfilled their dreams. As I walk in the presence of the wise, I will gleam from them. I have creative, insightful wisdom that challenges me to seek and possess the skills I need to live a successful life. With wisdom, I will tap into the goals and plans I will use to make my dream become reality. Wisdom is my guide into the future; therefore, I will inhale wisdom and exhale results.*

Meditate on your dream.

Review Progress:

1. What goals were completed?

2. What goals were not completed? Why not?

3. What distractions did you face today while pursuing your dream? How did you handle the distractions?

4. What type of bacteria tried to invade your environment? What solvent did you use to kill the bacteria?

5. Are you satisfied with the progress you made toward the fulfillment of your dream today? If so, why? If not, why?

Total hours spent towards fulfilling your dream_____

DREAM–FULFILLER'S REGIMENT

Day 16

Morning (6 to 6:10 a.m.):

Dream-fulfiller's Affirmation: *I choose to speak life into my dream. For my dream's sake, I choose to create a positive atmosphere in which it can properly grow and develop. When I face bumpy roads, I choose to speak life. When I face a never-ending road, I choose to speak life. When I feel disappointed, I choose to speak life. When I feel miserable, I choose to speak life. Life and defeat are in the power of the tongue. I choose to speak life.*

Meditate on your dream.
(Meditating is looking beyond your physical sight.)

Today's Goals:

1. _____

2. _____

3. _____

Midday (Noon to 12:10 p.m.):

Dream-fulfiller's Affirmation: *I choose to speak life into my dream. For my dream's sake, I choose to create a positive atmosphere in which it can properly grow and develop. When I face bumpy roads, I choose to speak life. When I face a never-ending road, I choose to speak life. When I feel disappointed, I choose to speak life. When I feel miserable, I choose to speak life. Life and defeat are in the power of the tongue. I choose to speak life.*

Meditate on your dream.

Evening (6 to 6:10 p.m.):

Dream-fulfiller's Affirmation: *I choose to speak life into my dream. For my dream's sake, I choose to create a positive atmosphere in which it can properly grow and develop. When I face bumpy roads, I choose to speak life. When I face a never-ending road, I choose to speak life. When I feel disappointed, I choose to speak life. When I feel miserable, I choose to speak life. Life and defeat are in the power of the tongue. I choose to speak life.*

Meditate on your dream.

Review Progress:

1. What goals were completed?

2. What goals were not completed? Why not?

3. What distractions did you face today while pursuing your dream? How did you handle the distractions?

4. What type of bacteria tried to invade your environment? What solvent did you use to kill the bacteria?

5. Are you satisfied with the progress you made toward the fulfillment of your dream today? If so, why? If not, why?

Total hours spent towards fulfilling your dream_____

DREAM-FULFILLER'S REGIMENT

Day 17

Morning (6 to 6:10 a.m.):

Dream-fulfiller's Affirmation: *I am a dream-fulfiller who recognizes not only the importance of criticism, but also my ability to put criticism in its proper place. Therefore, I will constantly discipline my feelings so they will not become vulnerable to criticism that is not conducive to the fulfillment of my dream. I will birth my dream into reality, so I will put criticism in its proper place.*

Meditate on your dream.
(You can tell what type of relationship a dream-fulfiller has with his dream based on the amount of time he meditates.)

Today's Goals:

1. _____

2. _____

3. _____

Midday (Noon to 12:10 p.m.):

Dream-fulfiller's Affirmation: *I am a dream-fulfiller who recognizes not only the importance of criticism, but also my ability to put criticism in its proper place. Therefore, I will constantly discipline my feelings so they will not become vulnerable to criticism that is not conducive to the fulfillment of my dream. I will birth my dream into reality, so I will put criticism in its proper place.*

Meditate on your dream.

Evening (6 to 6:10 p.m.):

Dream-fulfiller's Affirmation: *I am a dream-fulfiller who recognizes not only the importance of criticism, but also my ability to put criticism in its proper place. Therefore, I will constantly discipline my feelings so they will not become vulnerable to criticism that is not conducive to the fulfillment of my dream. I will birth my dream into reality, so I will put criticism in its proper place.*

Meditate on your dream.

Review Progress:

1. What goals were completed?

2. What goals were not completed? Why not?

3. What distractions did you face today while pursuing your dream? How did you handle the distractions?

4. What type of bacteria tried to invade your environment? What solvent did you use to kill the bacteria?

5. Are you satisfied with the progress you made toward the fulfillment of your dream today? If so, why? If not, why?

Total hours spent towards fulfilling your dream_____

DREAM-FULFILLER'S REGIMENT

Day 18

Morning (6 to 6:10 a.m.):

Dream-fulfiller's Affirmation: *I will respect my dream. I take full responsibility for those who come into contact with my dream. I choose to avoid people who intentionally try to suffocate the life out of my dream by their negative comments and/or sarcastic remarks. My circle of influence will consist of people who are capable and willing to speak life into my dream. I choose to associate with people who either will push me up or pull me up toward the level where my dream exists in the future.*

Meditate on your dream.
(Meditating day and night brings success.)

Today's Goals:

1. _____

2. _____

3. _____

Midday (Noon to 12:10 p.m.):

Dream-fulfiller's Affirmation: *I will respect my dream. I take full responsibility for those who come into contact with my dream. I choose to avoid people who intentionally try to suffocate the life out of my dream by their negative comments and/or sarcastic remarks. My circle of influence will consist of people who are capable and willing to speak life into my dream. I choose to associate with people who either will push me up or pull me up toward the level where my dream exists in the future.*

Meditate on your dream.

Evening (6 to 6:10 p.m.):

Dream-fulfiller's Affirmation: *I will respect my dream. I take full responsibility for those who come into contact with my dream. I choose to avoid people who intentionally try to suffocate the life out of my dream by their negative comments and/or sarcastic remarks. My circle of influence will consist of people who are capable and willing to speak life into my dream. I choose to associate with people who either will push me up or pull me up toward the level where my dream exists in the future.*

Meditate on your dream.

Review Progress:

1. What goals were completed?

2. What goals were not completed? Why not?

3. What distractions did you face today while pursuing your dream? How did you handle the distractions?

4. What type of bacteria tried to invade your environment? What solvent did you use to kill the bacteria?

5. Are you satisfied with the progress you made toward the fulfillment of your dream today? If so, why? If not, why?

Total hours spent towards fulfilling your dream_____

DREAM-FULFILLER'S REGIMENT

Day 19

Morning (6 to 6:10 a.m.):

Dream-fulfiller's Affirmation: *I am a dream-fulfiller who appreciates and respects the essence of time. I will work effectively and efficiently within the domain of time. I will use time wisely and not abuse the time that exists in my time frame. Within my time frame, I will be disciplined, diligent, focused and productive. When fulfilling my dream, I will not compare the timing of others' manifestation with mine. I acknowledge and accept that there is a proper time and procedure for my dream; therefore, I choose to respect time, and in return, time will respect me.*

Meditate on your dream.
(Meditation keeps you in pre-existing time while you wait for the future.)

Today's Goals:

1. _____

2. _____

3. _____

Midday (Noon to 12:10 p.m.):

Dream-fulfiller's Affirmation: *I am a dream-fulfiller who appreciates and respects the essence of time. I will work effectively and efficiently within the domain of time. I will use time wisely and not abuse the time that exists in my time frame. Within my time frame, I will be disciplined, diligent, focused and productive. When fulfilling my dream, I will not compare the timing of others' manifestation with mine. I acknowledge and accept that there is a proper time and procedure for my dream; therefore, I choose to respect time, and in return, time will respect me.*

Meditate on your dream.

Evening (6 to 6:10 p.m.):

Dream-fulfiller's Affirmation: *I am a dream-fulfiller who appreciates and respects the essence of time. I will work effectively and efficiently within the domain of time. I will use time wisely and not abuse the time that exists in my time frame. Within my time frame, I will be disciplined, diligent, focused and productive. When fulfilling my dream, I will not compare the timing of others' manifestation with mine. I acknowledge and accept that there is a proper time and procedure for my dream; therefore, I choose to respect time, and in return, time will respect me.*

Meditate on your dream.

Review Progress:

1. What goals were completed?

2. What goals were not completed? Why not?

3. What distractions did you face today while pursuing your dream? How did you handle the distractions?

4. What type of bacteria tried to invade your environment? What solvent did you use to kill the bacteria?

5. Are you satisfied with the progress you made toward the fulfillment of your dream today? If so, why? If not, why?

Total hours spent towards fulfilling your dream_____

DREAM–FULFILLER'S REGIMENT

Day 20

Morning (6 to 6:10 a.m.):

Dream-fulfiller's Affirmation: *I will not be dictated by anxious thoughts or feelings during the course of fulfilling my dream. The manifestation of my dream is the byproduct of patience and perseverance. Patience is a virtue; therefore, I acknowledge that fulfilling my dream is a process. I will not rush the process because there is a level of maturity that I will have gained while fulfilling my dream. I will be patient because good things come to those who wait.*

Meditate on your dream.
(Meditation provides a glimpse of yourself in the future.)

Today's Goals:

1. _____

2. _____

3. _____

Midday (Noon to 12:10 p.m.):

Dream-fulfiller's Affirmation: *I will not be dictated by anxious thoughts or feelings during the course of fulfilling my dream. The manifestation of my dream is the byproduct of patience and perseverance. Patience is a virtue; therefore, I acknowledge that fulfilling my dream is a process. I will not rush the process because there is a level of maturity that I will have gained while fulfilling my dream. I will be patient because good things come to those who wait.*

Meditate on your dream.

Evening (6 to 6:10 p.m.):

Dream-fulfiller's Affirmation: *I will not be dictated by anxious thoughts or feelings during the course of fulfilling my dream. The manifestation of my dream is the byproduct of patience and perseverance. Patience is a virtue; therefore, I acknowledge that fulfilling my dream is a process. I will not rush the process because there is a level of maturity that I will have gained while fulfilling my dream. I will be patient because good things come to those who wait.*

Meditate on your dream.

Review Progress:
1. What goals were completed?

2. What goals were not completed? Why not?

3. What distractions did you face today while pursuing your dream? How did you handle the distractions?

4. What type of bacteria tried to invade your environment? What solvent did you use to kill the bacteria?

5. Are you satisfied with the progress you made toward the fulfillment of your dream today? If so, why? If not, why?

Total hours spent towards fulfilling your dream_____

DREAM-FULFILLER'S REGIMENT

Day 21

Morning (6 to 6:10 a.m.):

Dream-fulfiller's Affirmation: *I am ready to push my dream into reality. I have a high tolerance for pain; therefore, I will not be intimidated by the discomfort I am currently experiencing. I will push my dream through the canal of becoming because my dream is destined to be in the land of existence. The time has come, so I must push.*

Meditate on your dream.
(Remember, it's your right to meditate.)

Today's Goals:

1. _____

2. _____

3. _____

Midday (Noon to 12:10 p.m.):

Dream-fulfiller's Affirmation: *I am ready to push my dream into reality. I have a high tolerance for pain; therefore, I will not be intimidated by the discomfort I am currently experiencing. I will push my dream through the canal of becoming because my dream is destined to be in the land of existence. The time has come, so I must push.*

Meditate on your dream.

Evening (6 to 6:10 p.m.):

Dream-fulfiller's Affirmation: *I am ready to push my dream into reality. I have a high tolerance for pain; therefore, I will not be intimidated by the discomfort I am currently experiencing. I will push my dream through the canal of becoming because my dream is destined to be in the land of existence. The time has come, so I must push.*

Meditate on your dream.

Review Progress:

1. What goals were completed?

2. What goals were not completed? Why not?

3. What distractions did you face today while pursuing your dream? How did you handle the distractions?

4. What type of bacteria tried to invade your environment? What solvent did you use to kill the bacteria?

5. Are you satisfied with the progress you made toward the fulfillment of your dream today? If so, why? If not, why?

Total hours spent towards fulfilling your dream_____

About the Author

Sheryl Brown lives in Central California. She is a Graduate of California State University, Bakersfield and holds a Bachelor of Science degree in Biology, Masters in Public Administration and a Master of Science in Psychology/Marriage Family Therapy.

Sheryl is also a Licensed Minister. She fulfills her mission by sharing the "Dream Fulfiller" process at conventions, seminars, and women's conferences throughout the United States.